Self-Publishing for Success

Every book deserves to be published

Second Edition

By

Alex Blackwell

Please Note:

Although in the course of this book we will refer to and may even recommend certain services or products, we have not received any incentives or sponsorship in any form from any service providers, suppliers or manufacturers. We also have no relationship with these entities, other than that we may avail of their services ourselves or use their products with the same rights and privileges as any other person, corporate or individual, may do. There may be other service providers, suppliers or manufacturers who provide equal or better services or products.

The advice that we provide here is based on our own experience and expertise. It is given without any prejudice, or any implied or other warranty.

The reader is advised to study and understand the terms and conditions of any service provider, supplier or manufacturer, whether we mention them or not, before entering into any agreement or contract with them.

ISBN Number: 9781793298911

To Daria,
who reminded me that for many years I had been
printing as well as self-publishing books and
that I should pass this experience along to others,
so that they might also craft something
that is meaningful and of importance to them
and be empowered to share their creation with others.

To Jeffrey
who introduced me to the printing industry
and taught me everything about it from ground up.

AB
Anno domini MMXIX

You don't have to be great
to start writing,
but you have to start
to be great at writing.

Zig Ziglar

Self-Publishing for Success

Every book deserves to be published

Second Edition

By

Alex Blackwell

Every Book Deserves to Be Published

As the saying goes, *everyone has a book in them*. Many have even written one in whole or in part. Most have given up as the publishing process proved either too daunting, or they were flatly rejected by either a literary agency or a publisher.

Experts in a particular field who are educators or have regular public speaking engagements may never even have considered writing a book or publishing. This happened to us with our first book (more on this later).

Then there are those who write just for the pleasure of it – titles never intended to sell a single copy. This may include a family history, a memoir or biography, a personal poetry collection, a photo album, or a cookbook just for distribution to friends and family for Christmas.

Taking "publishing" in its contemporary definition, all of these books deserve to be "published".

Where working with a commercial publisher is either impractical, impossible or undesirable, self-publishing or *publishing a book yourself, at your own expense*, is a viable option. In today's self-publishing world, the workflow from having written a book to holding a printed copy in your hand is the same, irrespective of whether you intend to print only one copy or produce the next best-selling blockbuster.

The ensuing pages will provide some insight into the self-publishing process including:

- How do you get to the point of being ready to publish your own work?
- How is a printed book produced?

- How do you create an eBook?
- How do you go about making a book available to readers?
- What does it take to market a book?
- How do you turn a book into a possible income stream – if that is indeed the objective?

The Traditional Route

Traditionally, an author would start by finding a literary agent to represent them in selecting and then negotiating a contract with a publisher. Alternatively, one might also approach a publisher directly.

Literary agents often have relationships with publishers and can make working with them much easier. For a percentage of the royalties[1], the agent negotiates the sale of all or a portion of the rights to a title with the publisher on behalf of the author. The rights can be broken down by geographic region and medium: print, digital, audio, film, etc. The rights can also be time limited.

Literary agents and publishers are, by and large, genre specific. That is, each will have one or a selection of genres for which they will accept proposals. The publisher we considered for our first book, for example, specialized in maritime fiction and non-fiction.

To get in through the door of an agency or a publishing house, the author must submit a proposal. Every agent/publisher wants the proposal formatted or laid out differently. They tend to be very specific in how this is to be done. Any deviation from their guidelines and a proposal may be rejected out of hand.

The proposal usually involves crafting a well-worded cover letter. It examines the competition in the intended segment and outlines how the title would fare in the market place. Then comes the book synopsis, where one describes the characters and plot in a very specific format. Finally, the package usually contains a writing

---

[1] The money an author receives for his or her work is called a "royalty". This is based on a percentage of the wholesale price per copy of the book sold but can also be an up-front fee paid by the publisher.

sample of up to fifty manuscript pages. Some accept only printed material, while others only accept digital submissions.

Whether one sends a submission to a literary agent or a publisher, it is often a frustrating experience. It may take them a month or much longer to look at a proposal. It is not deemed acceptable to send a proposal to more than one recipient at a time, so while one publisher or agent reviews your proposal, you should theoretically wait for their reply before sending one off to the next. The reply, when it does eventually come, is often an impersonal form letter. This leaves one wondering if anyone even read the proposal, or if the reader was just an intern charged with weeding out 99% of the submissions.

Many publishers state that they will not even consider titles that have already been self-published. We will look at this more closely in the following chapter.

The publisher we considered for our first book wanted to purchase it outright, which was one of the reasons we chose to self-publish it. His market was exclusively printed books sold in North America. He would then have been well within his rights to sell the foreign rights to a second publisher and the digital book rights to a third.

The purchase price we were offered by the publisher was based on a percentage of his net earnings per copy sold, multiplied by the number of books he intended to sell. This came to a tidy sum,[2] but there was a hitch. If the publisher did not sell the books as anticipated, he would have been able to claw back a portion of the royalties. On the other hand, if he sold more than the proposed quantity, we might have expected an additional payment – if, that is, he chose to print more.

---

[2] For more on how this works, please see chapter on Sales Models

Publishers should be viewed as business partners. They provide funding, expertise, co-ordination and guidance. They have in-house editors, designers and proof-readers who help the author. The publisher may choose to change the style, voice, layout and design of a book to fit into a line of other titles.

Once the book has reached a point where the publisher is satisfied, they will initiate the pre-sales marketing. This has several goals:

- To generate excitement about the upcoming title.
- To solicit reviews from known authorities for non-fiction titles or reputable people and publications for fiction, poetry, etc.
- To gauge the actual potential market for the book, which will help determine the number of books to be printed.

In our case, it was written into the contract that we would conduct speaking engagements and be available for book signings and interviews. The internet was not yet as established as it is today. Now author web pages, book specific blogs and a social media campaign will also be required of the author. Then even more publicity is pursued, such as radio and television interviews

If the book is the next blockbuster, then the publisher will fund most of this. If not, it is largely up to the author.

The publisher will then organize the printing and bindery of the books and send out the pre-release review copies. Larger publishers might have their own distribution operations. There are also major distributors specializing in warehousing books and getting them to the book-sellers.

A publisher's print run usually starts at about 10,000 copies. This depends on how they estimate the market.

That will also determine what their offer to the author will be. We were offered $10,000 for our book – based on $1 royalty per copy sold.

With the books printed and out for distribution, it is time for the actual marketing of the book. In the case of the lesser known author, this too falls on their shoulders. As above, the author will be expected to attend relevant meetings, do speaking engagements, book signings and conduct a continuous online campaign.

This work, along with the publisher's or distributor's sales force will create demand for your book and get it into the book shops where a customer may purchase it.

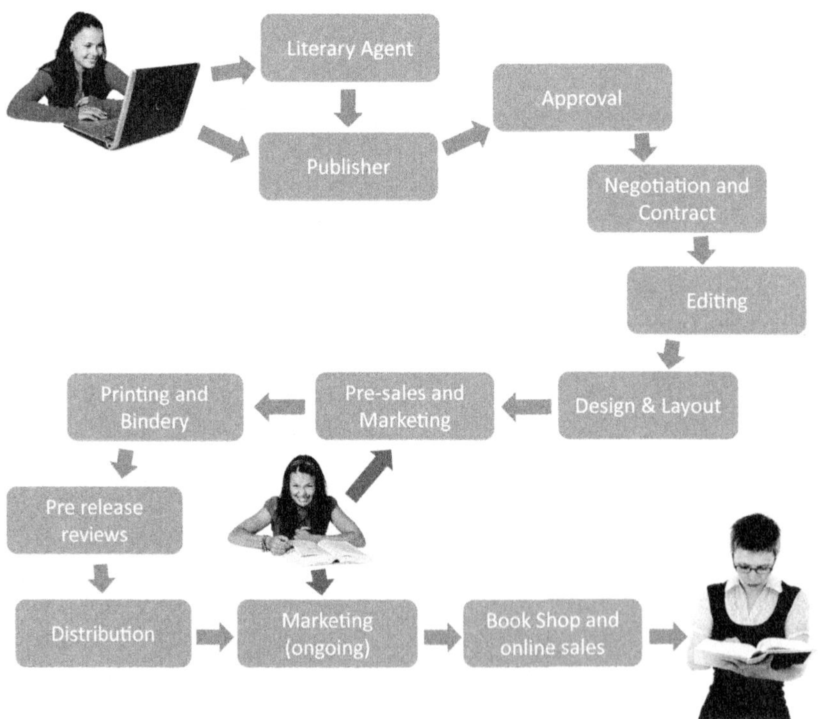

Then comes the not much spoken about question of "returns." Books that are not sold by a book-seller or are damaged in a shop, can be returned to the publisher.

The cost of this is then usually borne by the author – it is deducted from his or her royalties.

Self vs Traditional Publishing

Bearing in mind that most authors, including ourselves, would like the kudos attained in being accepted by a professional publisher:

Does self-publishing preclude an author from working with a traditional publisher down the line?

The answer to this perennial question is a resounding, "No"!

Beatrix Potter's story ***"The Tale of Peter Rabbit"*** was rejected by several publishers. In 1901 she self-published. A year later, Frederick Warne & Co, who had originally rejected the manuscript published it and 22 more of her books over the following 40 years.

Over two million Beatrix Potter books are sold each year.

Irma Rombauer wrote ***"The Joy of Cooking"*** with her daughter in 1931. Undeterred by the lack of interest, they printed 3,000 copies at $1.00 each and started selling them one at a time. Bobbs-Merrill Company subsequently acquired the rights.

The book has since sold over eighteen million copies.

In 1992 James Redfield self-published his first novel **"The Celestine Prophecy**." He drove around selling one copy at a time out of the boot of his car. Warner Books took note and purchased it.

The book became a Number One best-seller and has sold in excess of twenty million copies.

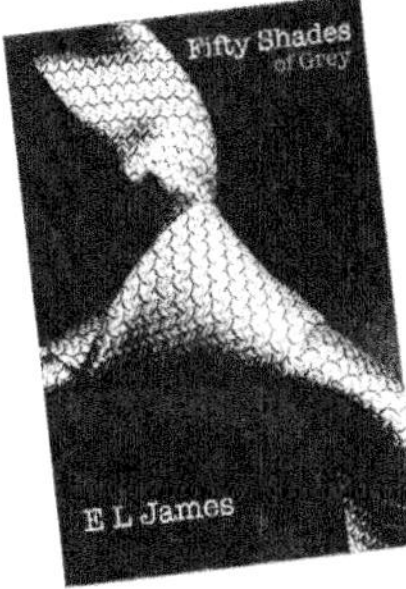

And then there is EL James. She was a best-selling author selling 250,000 copies of **"50 Shades"** via CreateSpace[3] before publishers even noticed her! She then went on to write **"50 Shades of Grey"** and self-published that as well. Vintage books then stepped in and acquired the rights.

She has now sold over seventy million copies of her "50 Shades" Trilogy worldwide!

So yes, there is hope for all as yet undiscovered authors. If your work is excellent and/or if you have proven that there is a market for your work, then it can make business sense for a publisher to take you on.

Then again, if your self-published book becomes that successful, perhaps you won't need a business partner.

---

[3] CreateSpace was a company for self-publishing books purchased by Amazon. Its capabilities have since been rolled over into Amazon's KDP (Kindle Direct Publishing).

Self-Publishing

Our First Book

Our first book came about more by accident than by design. We are sailors. Sailing is our antidote to the workday grind. While living and working in the US, we spent every free day sailing along the East Coast. In the evening we would drop anchor, enjoy the sunset over cocktails in a beautiful location – often parked in front of a multi-million-dollar mansion. Occasionally ‘things’ went wrong. Afterwards we would study what had happened and learn from the experience. We constantly upgraded our equipment and continued exploring.

One day we were chatting with fellow sailors, who remarked that they feared anchoring, being uncertain of their equipment and knowledge. They asked us to give a talk at our local club. Some time later we delivered a seminar at a major boat show. To our utter amazement, the large auditorium was packed. There were even people standing out in the hallway trying to listen to two amateurs talking about their experience.

After the seminar, an amazing ovation and a question session that went beyond our allotted time slot, we were inundated with requests to buy our book. “What book?” we countered and then we looked at each other.

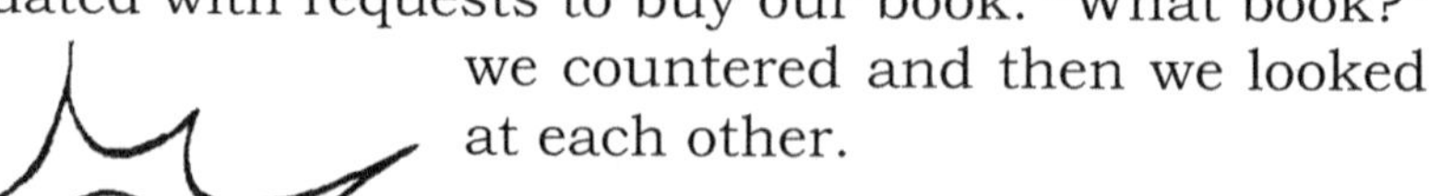

A light came on and we wrote “the book”.

It took us months of research and revisions to put down everything we thought a boater might need to know when it came to anchoring their boat. Yes, even such an obscure topic can provide a lot of material.

We wrote about the available equipment; categorizing and comparing all the major manufacturers' wares. We researched independent tests. We discussed techniques; and included anecdotes. "No, anchoring is not just throwing a heavy object overboard." Finally, we wrote about anchoring etiquette to liven things up a little. The result was: *Happy Hooking – the Art of Anchoring.*

At about that same time, I found myself at a book show. I was a co-owner of a commercial printing company and we were just developing a book printing division. We were there to meet publishers, book marketing companies and self-published authors; people who had a need for 50-1,000 copies of a given title.

There I met a publisher specializing in nautical titles. He offered us a nice up-front fee. However, the publisher wanted to change the title to something bland. We thought long and hard and finally declined the contract.

Another light came on. Why not self-publish? After all, I had a book printing business.

We printed 250 copies of our book and started down the self-publishing road. We became publishers in our own right!

The Downside of Self-Publishing

When opting to self-publish a title, you as the author accept the fact that you must ensure that everything is done. Yes, there are freelance editors, designers and marketers, who are available to help you with their expertise. Where you lack these skills, such services may be essential to bring a manuscript up to a standard at which people will want to read it.

You must also arrange for the books to be designed, formatted, printed and ultimately sold. To be sold, they first need to be packed and shipped to a reseller or reader. Self-publishing usually precludes you from using the major distributors, as they only deal with the big publishing houses. The sales channels for the self-published author are thus usually limited to online sales (print and/or digital) and to local book shops, where a personal connection may pave the way.

The Upside of Self-Publishing

Looking at the more positive side, you as a self-published author are empowered to be the *Master of Everything* to do with your work. Nobody else dictates anything. You determine how your book reads and for that matter how well it is edited. The look of the book – design and layout of the interior as well as the cover – all of this is entirely up to you to decide.

You are also the person who chooses how, where and if the book is to be sold. You may give away as many copies as you like. There is nobody, other than perhaps your bank manager, who has any say in this matter.

Any and all profit from the sale of every book goes exclusively to you as the author. Depending on the publishing model chosen, as a self-published author, you determine what the royalties are per copy sold.

In addition to that, the book or books become a legacy. The income stream built up over the years is something you will be able to leave behind for future generations to benefit from.

Self-Publishing Options

Once a title is written and edited, the contents are laid out and the cover is designed, there are two basic production and sales directions a self-published author may choose. Of course, a combination of the two is often also done.

Short Run Printing

Short run printing, as we did it in our shop, is the more traditional of the self-publishing options. Printers typically produce between 50 and 1,000 copies of a given title, either in soft cover (paperback) or hard cover. There are several available variations to the latter depending on what equipment the shop has. The books are then packed, and bulk shipped to the author or author's representative for sale or distribution.

In my printing business, when printing books for a publisher or marketing company representing an author, we were very careful to mask our company identity when we shipped orders out to their clients on their behalf. One author from Texas did manage to track us down. He phoned one morning, starting off the conversation by praising the excellent quality of the books we had printed.

"But there's just one problem," he continued.

My heart sank. If there was one thing, I dreaded, it was bad news first thing in the morning. It always bode ill for the rest of the day.

"What's that?" I asked cautiously, expecting the worst.

“It’s my living room,” he replied. “The whole room’s filled floor to ceiling with cartons.”

“Really?!” I exclaimed, suppressing a laugh, picturing the scene in my mind. I knew only too well how many cartons 1000 books came to, the standard order placed by his book marketing agency.

“Yeah!” he said by way of a reply, “Can y’all maybe print less if I send ya another book?”

“Sure,” I countered. “We routinely print as few as fifty copies.”

A month later he sent me the files for a novel he had just finished. We printed that and three more titles over the next few years. He was a happy customer.

The benefit of short run book printing is that you determine the quantity at the best available price for the number of books ordered. The downside is that you have to pay upon delivery before you’ve sold any books. You must also store the physical books and you must handle the packing and shipping when someone places an order. You also need to keep good track of financials, including revenue, tax where it is due and the costs of printing and shipping.

On Demand Printing

On demand printing or Print on Demand (POD) has gained a lot of traction in recent years. It is a fully automated book manufacturing system, where one copy of a given title is printed, bound and shipped at the time of the order. The benefits to the author are:

1. The author may order as many or as few books as are needed and only pay for the printing and shipping of these copies.
2. When it comes to sales, there is no upfront cost to the author for printing and shipping. The purchaser pays the online shop, the printer prints and ships and the online shop pays the author their royalty once a month.
3. There is no physical need to store books, nor pack, label and deliver them to the post office, saving time for writing.
4. There is no need to keep track of accounting. The online shop pays any tax in whatever jurisdiction the book is sold and reports year end revenue to you and the tax authorities.

The wonderful thing about POD is that once you have set up your account and uploaded and approved your book, there is nothing more to do other than check your bank balance. Of course, you must continually market and promote your book and yourself to keep it top of mind and high in the search rankings.

At our printing company, we looked into POD when we started producing books. It sounded very exciting and right up our alley. We made our way to the big printing equipment exhibition, having first registered our interest with the manufacturer in question. We were invited into the booth and were treated like royalty by the sales staff. The "booth" covered the area of a largish house. At the end of the tour, our excitement was huge – this was the wave of the future. Finally, the conversation came around to cost. The number quoted for the price of entry into on-demand book printing was staggering.

The first entrants into POD were already huge companies. For the next several years, we competed against them. Our selling point was quality, where we beat them hands down. Their advantage was the ability to print one-off books for large numbers of customers as they were ordered.

With the explosion of the internet and the vast improvement in the quality of the POD-produced books, this technology has found its niche. It has become very viable, with several big players.

Today there are also smaller POD machines such as the Espresso Book Machine, where one can have one or more copies of a soft cover book printed. These are targeted at Book shops, libraries, colleges or universities.

Ignoring the underlying technology somewhat, the process for an author is relatively simple[4]. Assuming that the book has been written, edited and rewritten to perfection, that the text pages have been laid out and that an eye-catching cover has been designed, it is just a matter of printing/exporting the text and cover to pdf and uploading it to the company selected to handle the

---

[4] The following notes are based entirely on KDP (Kindle Direct Publishing). Other suppliers will have similar interfaces and production flows. This will be described in greater detail in the chapter *Selling your Book Online Using KDP*.

printing. One such company is KDP (Kindle Direct Publishing), an Amazon company, with facilities in numerous countries, that handles the printing of books ordered from Amazon worldwide.

1. The first step is to create a new product entry on the supplier's web server. This includes all the physical information about how your book should be produced, descriptive information about the title and you (the author), the sales price and the sales channels. You then upload your pdf files (text and cover) to the supplier's web server.

   Once your files have been checked, there are options to view a digital proof or to order a printed proof. It is advisable to do both: first review the digital proof to make certain that nothing got lost in the translation from pdf to proof, then order a printed proof for review. It is important to look at the proof at least twice. Once to look at chapter headings, page layout and the likes to ensure that things haven't moved out of place or changed from expected styles. The second is to proofread the entire book one last time. We can guarantee that the eye will see things on paper that it missed on the screen.

   If everything looks good in the printed proof, then you may release the title, with which it is added to the Amazon catalogue.

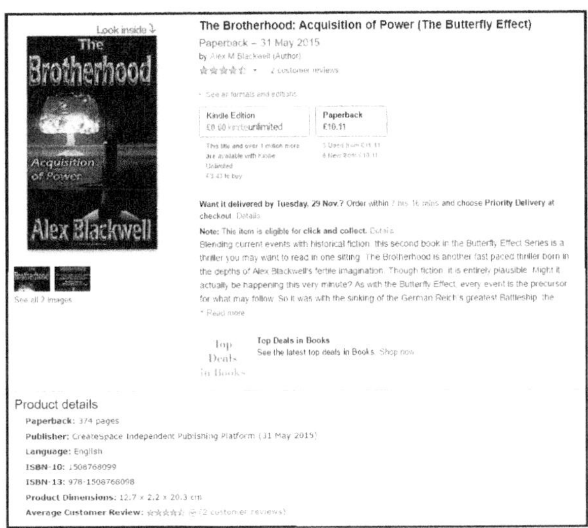

Amazon

2. Once your book has gone live, a potential reader may find it online. If and when they do and they like the look of your cover and your description, they may order your book.
3. Their order will trigger four parallel events:
    a. The book cover is printed, laminated and scored where it is meant to fold.
    b. The text pages are printed (=book block).
    c. A packing slip is printed.
    d. A shipping label is printed.
4. Then, without any further intervention, the cover and text pages are married up and glued together. The book is then three-knife-trimmed to the designated size.
5. The book is packed into a carton.
6. The packing slip is added, and the carton is sealed.
7. The shipping label is applied.
8. The package is sent off to your reader.

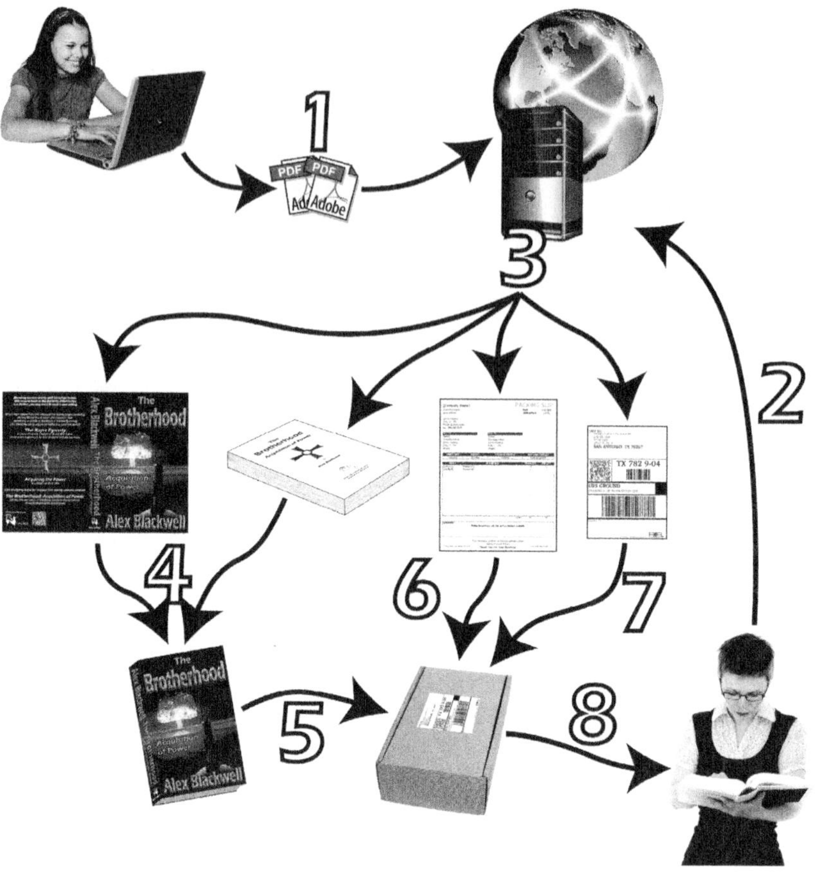

If your reader likes your book and writes a review, it will help generate further sales. We, therefore, add a request for a review to all our titles.

Writing Your Book

Until not too long ago – certainly within my life time – a manuscript was either handwritten or typed on a typewriter. This was then handed off to a publisher, who, besides editors, also had a type setter on staff who did the typography or type layout. Computers and word processing software changed everything.

We now all take software programmes such as Microsoft Word®, Apple Pages®, Google Docs®, OpenOffice®, or Adobe InDesign®, QuarkXPress®, as well as legacy programmes such as Adobe PageMaker® for granted. These applications enable anyone writing a text to format and lay out the words they craft as they go along. Of course, they may still hand off an unformatted manuscript to someone else.

What is important is that you, as the author, must have a feeling for where your strengths and weaknesses lie. We will endeavour to help you understand what is needed to "Do it yourself" or the DIY approach. Understanding what needs to be done should help you decide when to bring in help and how to work with someone else.

In most of the following examples we will also be going out from the assumption that most, if not all authors will preferentially be using Microsoft Word as opposed to a professional typesetting programme such as Adobe InDesign. InDesign is a very powerful piece of software, allowing the user to finesse the typography. It also allows a much wider range of image placement and text layout options. However, Word also has strong features, which make it more than adequate for you as an author. This book was written and laid out in Word.

Editing

"The first draft is just you telling yourself the story."

Terry Pratchett

Assuming that your book is written and that you have gone through several rounds of checking and rewriting, it is time for a fresh set of eyes to have a look.

When you consider just how many books are out there and that about 6,000 new titles[5] are published worldwide each and every day, there is no getting away from having to ensure that your book is the best that it can be. This includes proofreading and editing the text, laying it out and designing a good cover – the latter two items will be covered later on.

Say "Yes" to Editing

My first exposure to working with an editor came when I wrote my Master's thesis a good while ago. I spent two years conducting practical research, then collecting and interpreting mountains of data.

Finally, my manuscript was done. I had poured my heart and soul into this document. It was the most precious thing I had ever created. I knew it was a perfect masterpiece.

A close friend of my parents offered to read my work. This was still in the days before computers and word processors, so I handed him my precious, typewritten

[5] Aproximately 2,200,000 book titles are published each year https://en.wikipedia.org/wiki/Books_published_per_country_per_year

manuscript; the only copy in existence. A few weeks later he returned my document.

When I opened it and flipped through the pages, my heart sank. Almost every line on every page was marked up in glaring red ink. To say that I was devastated would be a huge understatement. I wanted to cry. I wanted to burn the wretched pages. My greatest achievement, the culmination of years of work was rubbished by this so-called "friend".

I threw my thesis in a corner and went for a walk – a very long walk. I was distraught. I had always had a suspicion that I was a fraud, that the academic goal I had set for myself was way beyond my reach.

Hours later (it might have been days) I returned. The manuscript was still lying there. I looked at it, wishing it would vanish. Miserable to the core, I reached out and picked it up. I started at page one and began to read.

There was a short note at the top from the friend saying that he had been amazed by the scope and quality of what I had written. Because of this he had taken particular pains in critiquing it and making suggestions.

I read on. Word by word and line by line, I compared my writing with his comments. I was awestruck with the depth and understanding with which he had treated my meagre efforts. I pulled out my typewriter and started to write from scratch. There were suggestions that caused me to rethink whole sections and the occasional one, that after some thought, I dismissed.

Several months and two more rewrites later I handed the final printed and bound book in to my professor. He was ecstatic. In no small part because of my editor, my thesis became the foundation of decades of subsequent research work and was widely cited.

Since then I have written short stories, fiction thriller novels and non-fiction 'how-to' books. Each time, as with any other author, my writing has been a bearing of my soul – irrespective of what had been written. Writing is an intensely personal experience. It is connected to the fragile inner psyche. Still, each time, I bite the proverbial bullet and hand that which is nearest and dearest to my heart off to my editor.

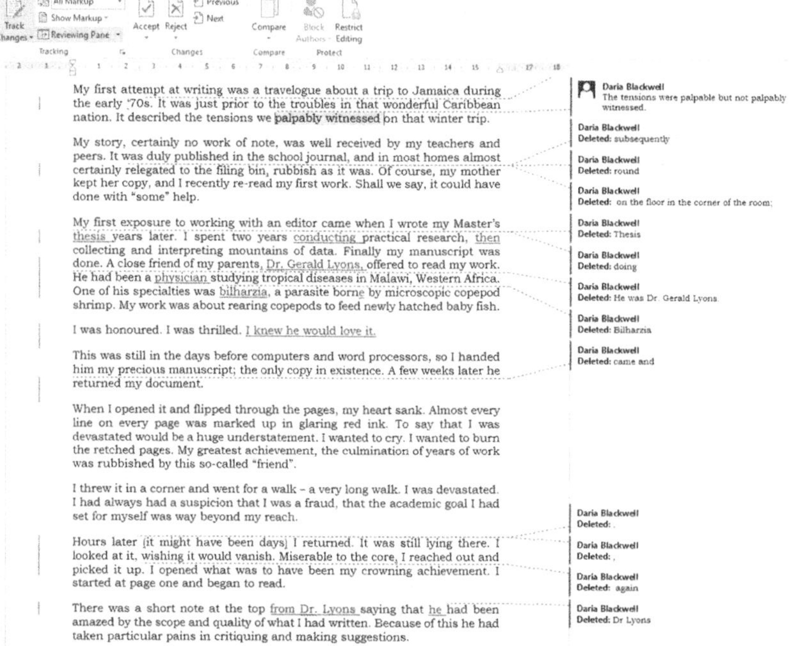

My first attempt at writing was a travelogue about a trip to Jamaica during the early '70s. It was just prior to the troubles in that wonderful Caribbean nation. It described the tensions we palpably witnessed on that winter trip.

My story, certainly no work of note, was well received by my teachers and peers. It was duly published in the school journal, and in most homes almost certainly relegated to the filing bin, rubbish as it was. Of course, my mother kept her copy, and I recently re-read my first work. Shall we say, it could have done with "some" help.

My first exposure to working with an editor came when I wrote my Master's thesis years later. I spent two years conducting practical research, then collecting and interpreting mountains of data. Finally my manuscript was done. A close friend of my parents, Dr. Gerald Lyons, offered to read my work. He had been a physician studying tropical diseases in Malawi, Western Africa. One of his specialties was bilharzia, a parasite borne by microscopic copepod shrimp. My work was about rearing copepods to feed newly hatched baby fish.

I was honoured. I was thrilled. I knew he would love it.

This was still in the days before computers and word processors, so I handed him my precious manuscript; the only copy in existence. A few weeks later he returned my document.

When I opened it and flipped through the pages, my heart sank. Almost every line on every page was marked up in glaring red ink. To say that I was devastated would be a huge understatement. I wanted to cry. I wanted to burn the retched pages. My greatest achievement, the culmination of years of work was rubbished by this so-called "friend".

I threw it in a corner and went for a walk – a very long walk. I was devastated. I had always had a suspicion that I was a fraud, that the academic goal I had set for myself was way beyond my reach.

Hours later (it might have been days) I returned. It was still lying there. I looked at it, wishing it would vanish. Miserable to the core, I reached out and picked it up. I opened what was to have been my crowning achievement. I started at page one and began to read.

There was a short note at the top from Dr. Lyons saying that he had been amazed by the scope and quality of what I had written. Because of this he had taken particular pains in critiquing and making suggestions.

Daria Blackwell
The tensions were palpable but not palpably witnessed.

Daria Blackwell
Deleted: subsequently

Daria Blackwell
Deleted: round

Daria Blackwell
Deleted: on the floor in the corner of the room;

Daria Blackwell
Deleted: Thesis

Daria Blackwell
Deleted: doing

Daria Blackwell
Deleted: He was Dr. Gerald Lyons.

Daria Blackwell
Deleted: Bilharzia

Daria Blackwell
Deleted: came and

Daria Blackwell
Deleted: .

Daria Blackwell
Deleted: ,

Daria Blackwell
Deleted: again

Daria Blackwell
Deleted: Dr Lyons

A page of a Word document with editorial comments

From my original editor and true friend, who graced an insignificant youth with his expertise, I learned that all important lesson:

As an author it is my role to have an idea and to paint a picture with words. It is the editor's job to see my idea and make my work the best it can be. This is a delicate but immensely valuable partnership.

That was how I learned just how vital it is to have one's work edited.

Rule #1: You cannot properly edit or proof your own work.

I'm not saying you should not read, re-read, rewrite and keep changing things in your manuscript – that is also proof reading and editing. What you cannot do is find all the spelling errors (typos), grammatical errors, inconsistencies, word duplications, idiosyncrasies, flow errors, etc. Having composed a document, your mind reinterprets what you have written and thus misses many things. This is perfectly normal and does not make you a poor writer.

In our printing company, we routinely printed brochures and newsletters written by our clients. "Yes, the text is perfect," I was always told. We did the design and layout. When I read the copy provided, I invariably stumbled over items including typos, improper punctuation, grammar and word usage. Very commonly I would find there was something missing, or that I could not understand the point. That was often caused by an omission by the author, where they had either assumed the reader would know this or that, or worse, where the writer had thought that the item had been included while it was not – even after many edits on their part.

We added a proof reader and an editor to our staff and were able to add additional services to our portfolio.

Yes – editing can be expensive.

When hiring someone for any task you will usually pay them an hourly rate for their work. Editing is no different. For basic copy editing, the published guideline is 30-40 dollars or euros per hour. An editor will typically cover 3-5 manuscript pages an hour. Multiplying that with the length of your document will give you have a rough idea of overall cost. (200 pages would come to approximately $1,500-2,000.) If the editor needs to do a lot of work, they will cover fewer pages per hour and your costs will go up commensurately.

When it comes to having your book edited, there are, of course, several things you can and probably should do before you pass your book on to an editor. Just think of the adage that *"Time is Money".* The less time an editor needs to spend fixing things, the less you will have to pay for this service.

Tip!

Writing Tips

Retain consistency while writing

Readers will invariably notice detail or plot consistency mistakes. You can avoid this by keeping track of details about characters, locations, time lines and so on in spreadsheets.

Alex Blackwell

The Tenth Plague					
Chapter	Setting	Characters	Summary	Outcome	Time
Prologue	Mine, Ishpeming	Rutherford Wils	Willa flees mine disaster.	Wils survives, remembers what his friend found.	Nov. 1926
Some Day in May Part 1: The Writing on the Wall					
1	Courtroom	Gillian and Marc	Thayers attend hearing to get rights of adopted baby	She fears someone may try to take her baby away	May, some day
2	Compound in San Antonio	Cyrus	Cyrus visits his son's grave.	He makes plans for revenge.	May, someday
3	Hotel Room	Gillian and Marc	Gillian loads photos of the baby to Facebook.	She sees Gabriel in Facebook, remembers bad memories..	
4	Alex's Grave	Cyrus	Cyrus reviews plans.		
Two Months Later, July, Thursday					
Plague 1: Blood					
5	Bathroom at SRCC	Brianne Hyde	Brianne Hyde washes hands when water turns to blood.	Brianne escapes, puzzled by what happened.	July, morning
6	Highway, Tahoe	Gillian and Marc	Gillian wakes from a nightmare. The Thayers drive to the resort.	Marc agrees to give his BlackBerry to G.	8:30 a.m.
7	Plantation-style house	Lacey Caruthers	Lacey can't reach her husband. She interacts with Sammy.	Lacey sees mud on Sammy's shoes and wonders where he wandered off to.	9 a.m.
8	Tahoe, resort	Gillian	The Thayers arrive to find protestors.	The receptionist encourages them to ask Jared about the cause of the fuss.	10 a.m.
Plague 2: Frogs					
9	Jared's suite	Jared Russo	Jared has been poisoned.	Jared dies.	11 a.m.
10	Thayers' suite	Gillian and Marc	They find their suite and hear screams.	Marc goes to see what's wrong.	Noonish
11	Resort hallways	Marc	Marc explores the source of screams.	Marc finds the body of Jared Russo.	12:15 p.m.
12	Resort hallways, security office	Cyrus	Cyrus finds security office and accesses it.	Austin takes the surveillance video.	12:30 p.m.
13	Suite	Gillian and Marc	The Thayers talk to Sheriff Griswold.	Vernon knocks on door and wants to talk to them.	1 p.m.

Adam Blumer

Avoid abusing adverbs

In describing a situation or a scene, try to avoid using words ending in "ly". My most common one is "simply." It is a word that is almost always simply ☺ unnecessary. As a matter of course, I now do a search and replace on each finished document for this word.

Formatting

As mentioned elsewhere in more detail, stick to 'styles'. The body text should all be the same style: "Normal" in Word.. Mixing styles not only looks bad but can be hard to read. Add formatted titles and Chapter headings as needed: Heading 1, 2 3... in Word. Include a table of contents for eBooks[6], even if your printed book does not need one.

To change how a text element looks, modify the style. Do not format the text.

---

[6] Note that the Word generated table of contents is recommended for Kindle, but not for Smashwords

Punctuation

Improper comma usage is a very common mistake that can ruin an enjoyable read. There is one caveat: US English and British English have differing rules, so knowing your primary audience/market is important. For example, in British English the end punctuation always appears outside closing quotation marks. In American English, it appears inside.

The proper use of the period, hyphen, colon and semi-colon are also very important. Used correctly they can make for a pleasant read. Run-on sentences usually do not; though we do know of one award winning novel that has no periods.

*"Panda. Large black-and-white bear-like mammal, native to China. **Eats, shoots and leaves.**"*

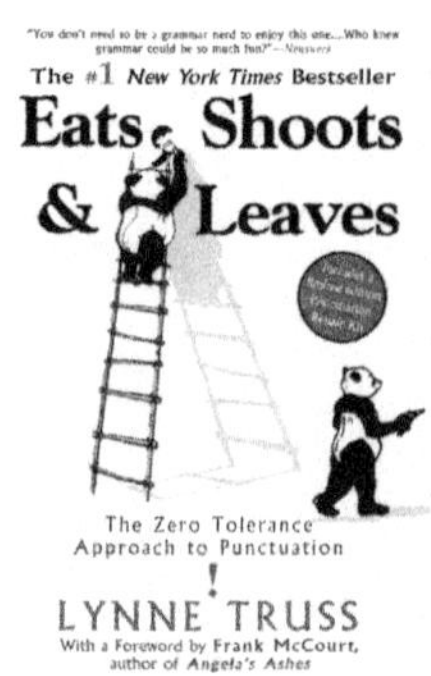

Because of a misplaced comma after the word “Eats”, when the poor panda went somewhere to eat, it was then forced shoot everyone, prior to leaving.

Grammar

Unless you are a grammar expert, keep it simple. Errors that you may not notice will put readers off reading your work. Pay attention to your software's editorial flags. There are free online grammar checkers, like grammarly.com, that you can utilize as a cross check.

Grammar is the difference between:
"knowing your shit"
and
"knowing you're shit"!

Structure

A story should have a beginning, a middle and an end. Some excitement or tension at the beginning will get a reader interested in continuing. Knowing where your book ends will help you build the middle without giving away too much about the ending.

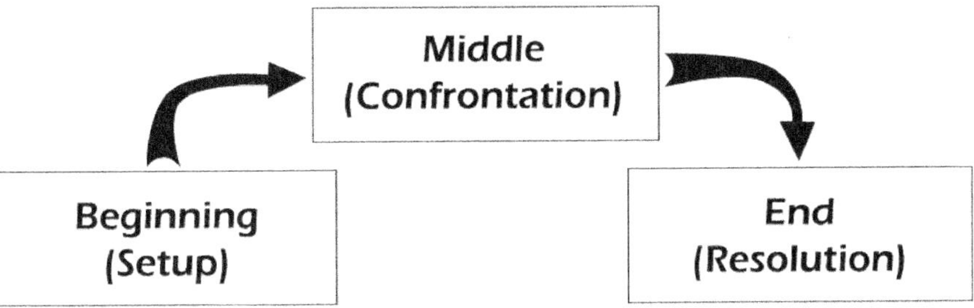

Similarly, with a non-fiction title, try to develop the book methodically, without repetition. If there is a logical flow, it will be easier to read and understand.

Tense

Changing tense in a book, unless you are describing something that happened prior to the story, is very confusing. Keep the tense consistent.

Person

When writing the narrative, choose either first person where you are describing things, or third person, where you are listening to someone else describe what is happening. (Using second tense is very rare.) Mixing these is confusing to the reader.

Read out loud

Reading out loud and intoning what you are reading, particularly dialogue, is a great way to read your work as if you were another person. You will stumble over mistakes and sentences that just don't work. You can also hear your characters' voices and get a feel for what they should or should not sound like.

Cut unnecessary text

Having crafted and wordsmithed your masterpiece, cutting is perhaps the hardest thing to do. As you read your manuscript, look at every sentence and paragraph critically. Over-explanation, over-writing and repetition are easy pitfalls. Ask yourself, "Is this important?" Can the story do without it? Trust your reader to remember what you wrote and eliminate repetition, which is boring.

If there is any doubt,
"Leave it out".

Just think Hemmingway or Conrad. Both wrote the most beautifully crafted novels. Most of their books are a short read, in which each word is perfect. An author of a book should take the time to cut, cut and cut some more.

Proof reading

Having completed the preceding steps and done them more than once, it is time to let someone else look at your work. This is the time to start swallowing your pride and let others in to your world.

By all means start with family and friends if they are skilled and willing. Ask them for written suggestions. Do not look over their shoulder while they read your work. Impersonal is more honest and should not lead to antagonistic episodes. Accept their suggestions with gratitude. Then make changes as you see fit – it is your work and you may disagree. Find a peer for objective and constructive feedback. You might also try crowd sourced editing – see following.

Accept all the feedback – even if critical. Remember the book is your creation; it's your baby and you are vulnerable and wanting to protect it. Objective criticism is of your work, not of you. It will help you catch inconsistencies and fix plot mistakes. Don't listen selectively where you want to; really consider all the feedback thoughtfully. It will help make your work much better.

Crowd sourced editing

We first tried this with our non-fiction book on boat anchoring (*Happy Hooking – the Art of Anchoring*). When we had completed writing and editing the manuscript ourselves, we sent it out to anchor manufacturers in several countries. Though not always positive, their response was very constructive. The result is that the book has been the best-selling title in its (small) genre for years.

Our second foray into crowd sourced editing was my first novel (*The Butterfly Effect; It started on 9/11*). We sent free digital copies to willing reviewers on our social media sites and our mailing list. We received many good edits, corrections and comments. They were not always easy for the reviewer to write and not always easy to accept, yet the input greatly improved the book. It takes bravery to put your work out there and ask for criticism.

Start back at the beginning

Put your book away for a while. Do something else for a few days or a few weeks. Then start reading it word for word from the beginning. You will be surprised at how many small mistakes you catch and how many paragraphs you can polish to flow even better. You will likely also find sections that need to be swapped around and even parts missing altogether. Some of the greatest authors the world has ever known were renowned for making changes in every subsequent printed edition.

Setting up your book

Unless the reader knows you personally or you are a well-known personality, how your book looks is almost as important as what has been written.

Book dimensions

Give the actual size of your book some thought before moving on to the next sections.

Size does matter

Ask yourself some important questions:

- What is the purpose of your book?
- How will a reader handle it?
- Is it a pocket book or a coffee table book?
- Will it fit on a book shelf?
- What size is the norm for the genre you are writing in?

There are a number of industry standard book sizes. A cost factor is what fits best on a sheet of paper that is run through a printing press. In self-publishing, this is usually a digital press. Another factor is what fits best on a shelf in a bookshop.

After a book has been printed it is cut or trimmed to its final size. This is called “trim size”.

Stick to Industry Standard Trim-Sizes

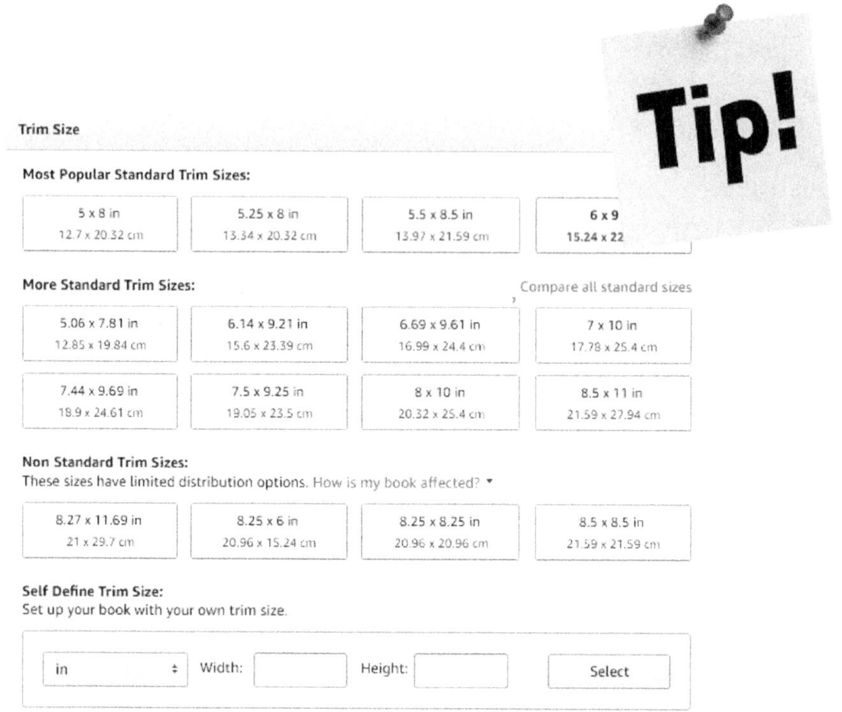

Of course, you may select a non-standard size. Because this may not fit as well on the press sheet, the paper usage can be less efficient. It may also require additional work to produce. It may therefore cost you more.

Interior

The design and layout of the interior pages of your book will help determine its readability and the book's page count.

Note: The page count (and size) directly affects the production cost of the book. Printing more pages or larger pages costs more, thereby increasing the price of your book to buyers or decreasing your margin to make it saleable.

Book templates (MS Word) are available on KDP and from other resources such as on our website. We have published a page with links to some common book sizes and much other useful information. Go to: whiteseahorse.ie/books

Our templates are easily downloaded and simple to use. They are sized to the standard trim sizes and include placeholders for most of the components you might want to have in your book. The type styles (see below) are properly set up and the margins are correctly mirrored.

Page Setup

Once the size (dimension) of the book has been determined, the margins need to be defined – if you are not using a template file. In a book, you will select mirrored margins as in the shown example (this book).

The Live area is typically ¼ inch in from the trim size. No text should go outside the live area. This area from the edge of the page is called the 'margin'. With mirrored pages the inside margin or gutter increases to ½ inch to allow for the glue and also for how the pages in a bound book come together because of the book spine. The top and bottom margins are both increased respectively to accommodate the header and footer.

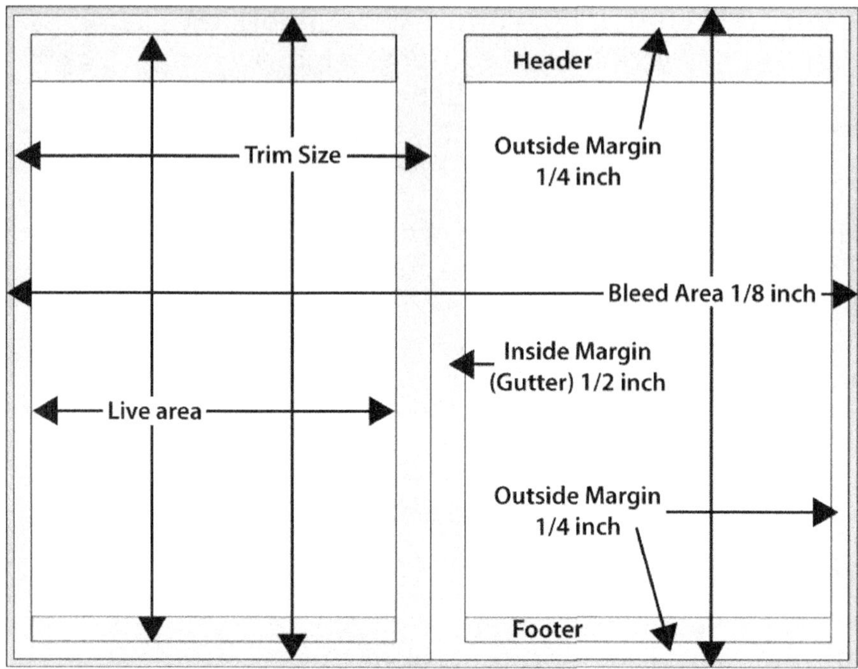

The bottom margin is typically used for the page number, while the top margin often has the book title and author name – as was done in this book.

If there are images in the book and if it is intended that they extend to the edge of the page, then they should actually extend to the edge of the bleed area - 1/8 inch beyond the trim. This is to allow for 'bounce' when the page is trimmed.

Note that when viewing the pages in two-page layout in MS Word the odd numbered page is displayed on the left, while, when printed, it is actually the right-hand page. In a page layout programme like Adobe InDesign or OpenOffice, this is displayed as one will actually see it in the printed book with the facing pages (reader's spreads) facing each other. This is not the case in the MS Word 2-page layout view.

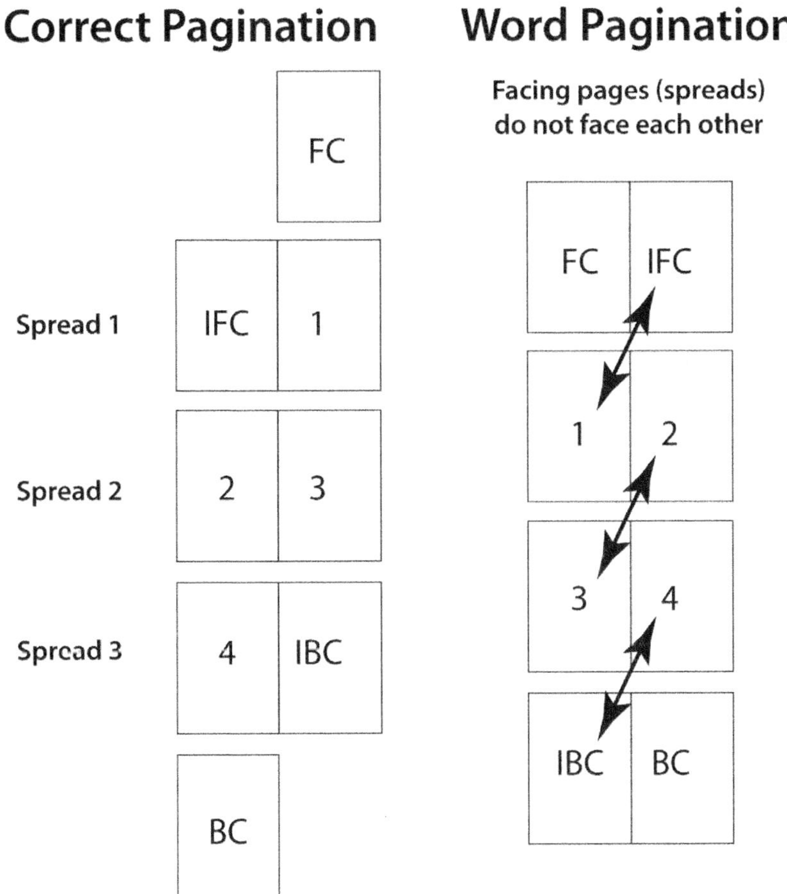

Page Layout

Much of the actual page layout is up to the designer. There are many things one can choose from to personalize the look of a book. Some options include single or multiple column layout, line spacing, line justification, paragraph spacing, indenting the first line of a paragraph, drop-caps at a chapter beginning and the list goes on.

Book Sections

Books will typically be divided into three sections: The **Front Matter** contains information about the book, the **Book Body** is the text of the book and the **End Matter** will contain further information supporting the book, plus other elements the author or publisher may wish to include. Here is a list of some of the types of elements these front and end book sections may include.

Front Matter

- Half Title (Sometimes Called Bastard Title)
- Copyright Page with ISBN number
- Dedication
- Acknowledgments
- Frontispiece (Illustration facing the title page)
- Title Page title of the book, the author (or authors) and the publisher[7]
- About the Author (can also be in the back)
- Table of Contents
- Foreword
- Preface or Introduction

End Matter

- Glossary
- Bibliography
- Index
- About the Author (can also be in the front)
- Further reading
- Also by this Author or Publisher

---

[7] It is often desirable to create a graphic (picture) for the title page. If you do this, it will maintain its look and feel when converting to an eBook. For help with this see the section: Creating an image from a Word or Excel document

Typography

When writing any text in Word, it is very tempting to just make the type size bigger and bolder or to change the font to make a chapter head. You might also be tempted to do this to emphasize something. Don't dismay, almost everyone does this, because they do not know any better.

Instead:

Strictly adhere to styles

Almost all typesetting programmes offer a wide range of pre-set type-styles. It is very important to make a habit of strictly using these styles. If by chance there is no type-style matching your needs, you are free to create as many more styles as you choose.

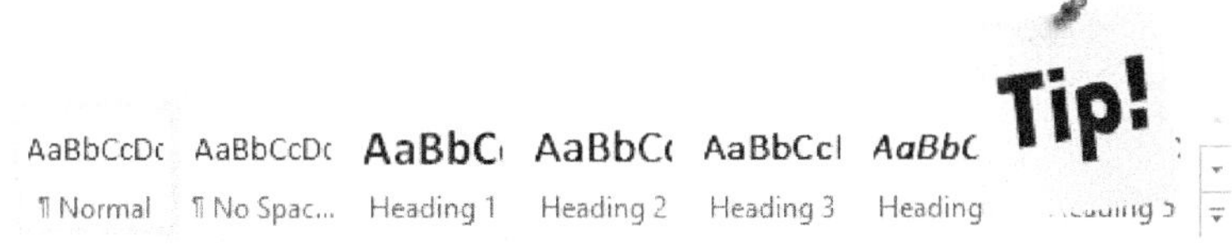

Microsoft Word® type-styles menu bar

Misusing type-styles or changing font characteristics in the text may work ok with the printed book, but is very likely to produce unexpected results when doing the eBook conversion. To repeat: **Make a habit of always strictly adhering to type-styles.**

The type-styles you will most commonly use are:

Normal (**Default** in Open Office): Use this and only this for your body text. Italics and Bold are allowed for emphasis. You may also right-justify or centre specific text elements as needed. Nothing else.

Heading 1, 2, 3...: These are intended for Chapter headings, subheads, etc. Do not use them for anything else, as this will later be misinterpreted when you convert your book to an eBook.

Title, Caption, Quote, etc.: There are many other pre-determined styles to choose from. You may also create additional styles as needed.

The beauty of using styles becomes evident when you decide to change how your book looks. For example, if you want to change the font of your body text, then all you need to do is modify the style 'Normal' in Word or 'Default' in Open Office.

This will become of particular importance if/when you decide to convert your book to an eBook format such as Kindle[8]. In eBooks, how letters and symbols are displayed is coded into the file using what is called a mark-up language. Web pages use this in the same way. Online they use html, or Hyper Text Mark-up Language. The text styles (in MS Word) translate smoothly into html and similar formats.

If you apply formatting or text effects other than bold or italics in the document, these will be ignored in translation to an eBook. In many cases, they may also not print out in the final book the same way as they appear on screen. WYSIWYG (What you see is what you get) does not always apply.

Similarly, avoid using fancy, non-standard fonts. First of all, they do nothing for your book and may actually detract from its readability. More important, they often do not have proper font metrics, which are descriptions on how the font should print and how the individual characters relate to each other. Finally, the e-reader

---

[8] We describe this process in some detail later on

(Kindle or other) will, in all likelihood not have this font loaded and will thus not be able to display it.

If you wish to change the way a font displays in your document[9] (apart from bold and italics), then modify the style, do not change it in the running text of the document. This will automatically change each occurrence of this style – saving you a lot of work or money down stream.

To change the way your text looks, right-mouse-click the type-style you want to modify and then left-mouse-click: "Modify":

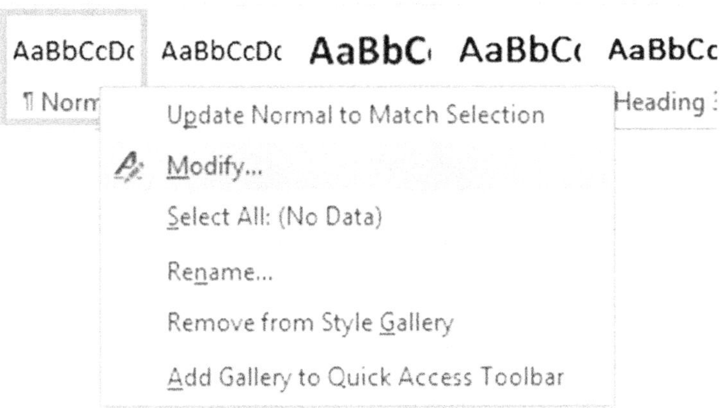

This will bring you to a page where you can change a number of the characteristics of how the characters of the type-style will appear in your book. These include:

- Font
- Size
- Bold, Italic, etc.

[9] Note, however, that style changes may not be picked up by the Kindle device, or other viewer.

This window also allows you to make some changes to how the paragraph is formatted, such as justification/alignment, line spacing etc. It is, however, advised to do this on the 'Modify Paragraph' page instead. Please see below for more detail on this.

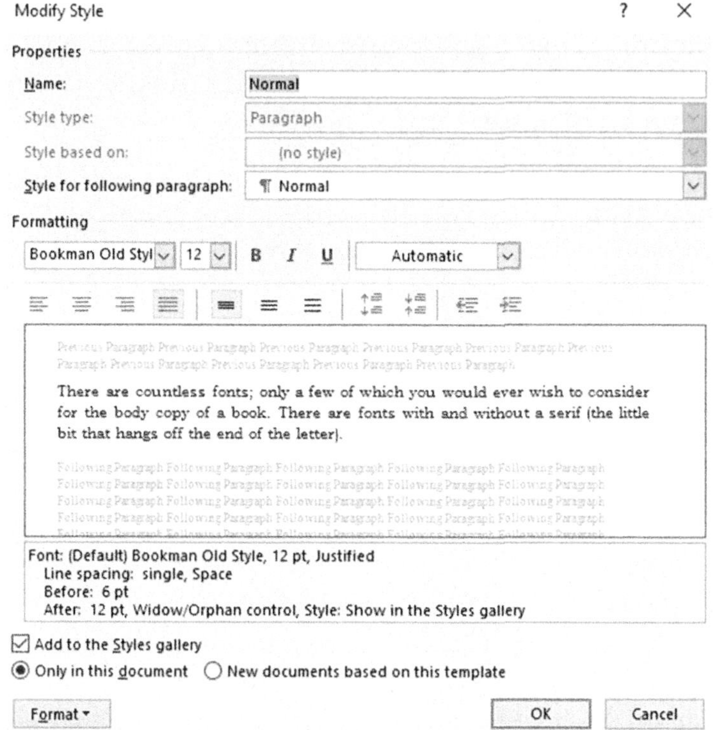

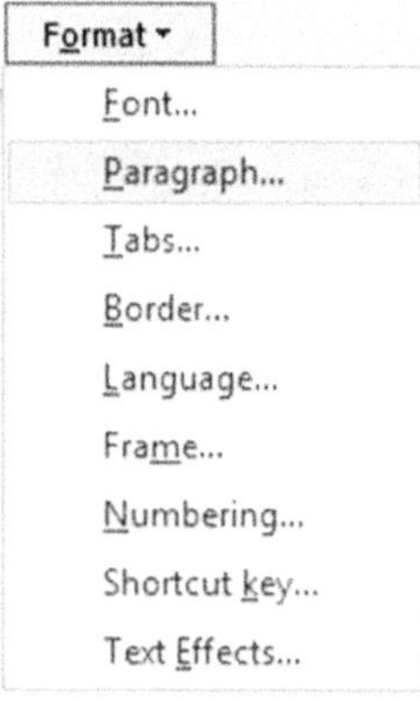

To change the characteristics of how a paragraph looks when assigned a particular style, click on the 'Format' button on the bottom left corner of this window.

In the drop-down menu select 'Paragraph'.

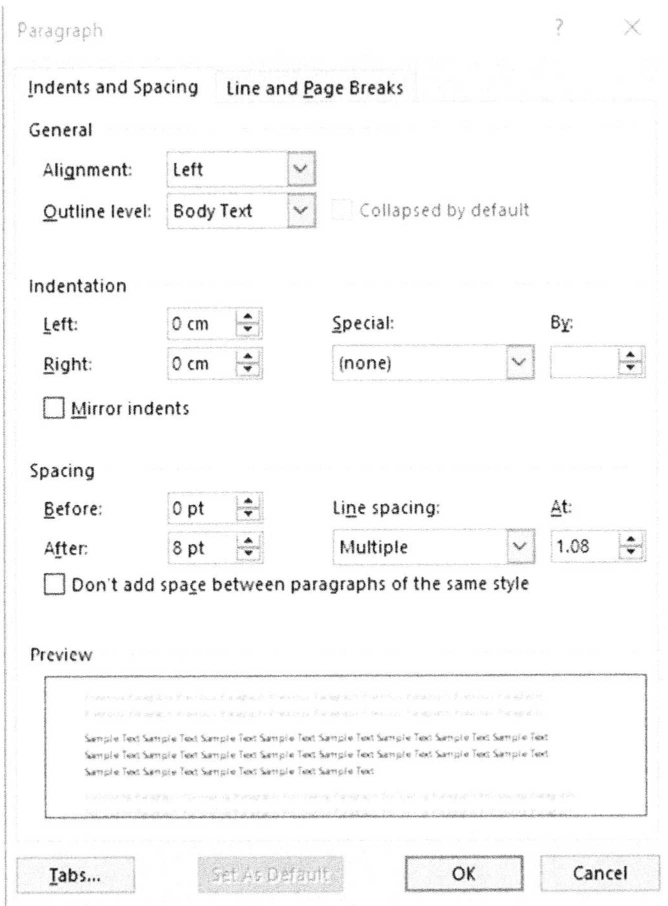

In this window you can change the way a paragraph appears in your type-style. If you want the first line of a paragraph indented, this is done under 'Indentation' and 'Special'. Select First Line and enter the desired indent amount to the right.

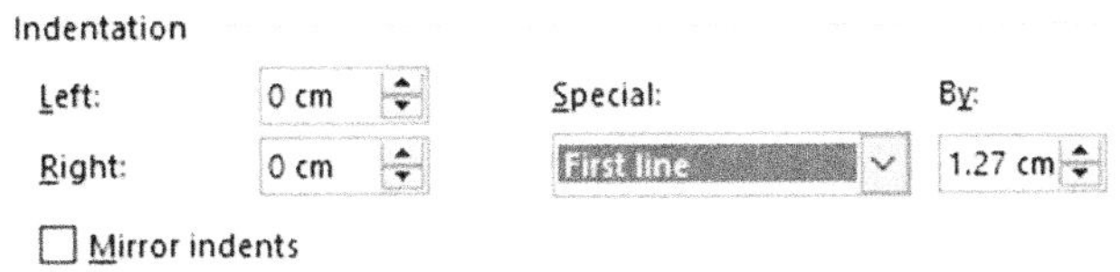

This is also where you can add some space after a paragraph and determine the desired line spacing. For unformatted manuscripts this is often 'double'. In this book it is ‘single’ and if you wish to open the spacing up a bit, you can enter whatever number you desire. In typesetting the line spacing is called ‘leading’.

The other tab under ‘Paragraph’ is ‘Line and Page Breaks.

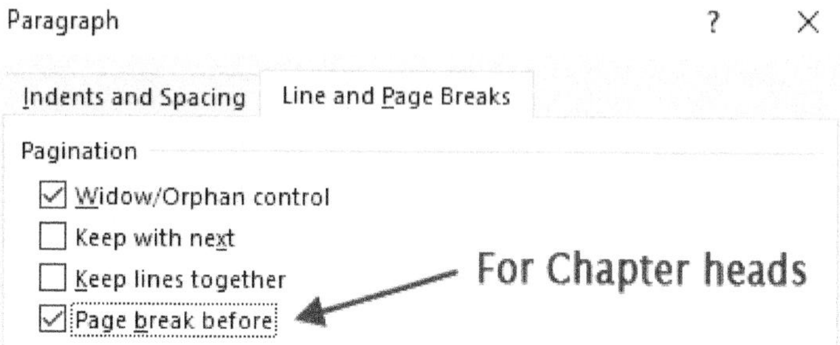

If you would like to start each chapter on a new page, then for the Heading type-style you are using for your chapter heads, check ‘Page break before’.

Widows and Orphans

The ‘Widow/Orphan control’ is of particular relevance to the style ‘Normal’. In most instances, you will want to ensure it is checked for this type-style.

Writing guides, such as the *Chicago Manual of Style*, generally suggest that a manuscript should have no widows and orphans, even if the result of avoiding them is additional space at the bottom of a page or column. A *widow* is a paragraph-ending line that falls at the beginning of the following page or column, thus separated from the rest of the text. An *orphan* is a paragraph-opening line that appears by itself at the bottom of a page or column, thus separated from the rest of the text.

MS Word can do a good job of avoiding widows and orphans. To ensure this is done, right mouse click the style 'Normal'.[10] Left mouse-click on 'Format' and select 'Paragraph'. Then click on the 'Line and Page Breaks' tab. Finally, ensure that 'Widow/Orphan control' is checked.

Difficulty changing the style of some text

With documents that have seen a lot of work, or where there has been cutting and pasting from other documents or sources, there is sometimes difficulty in applying a style to a text element. You have two options to get around this.

1 Highlight the offending text. Click on the little down arrow at the bottom right corner of the Style selection box:

[10] All body text should be using the 'Normal' style. Please see the beginning of this section on Typography.

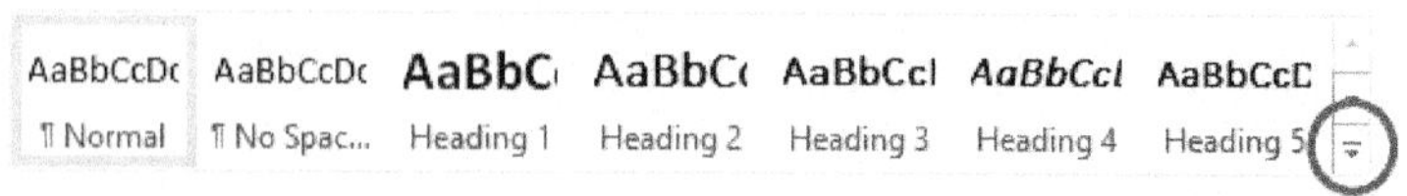

This will expand the style selection box. Now click on 'Clear Formatting'.

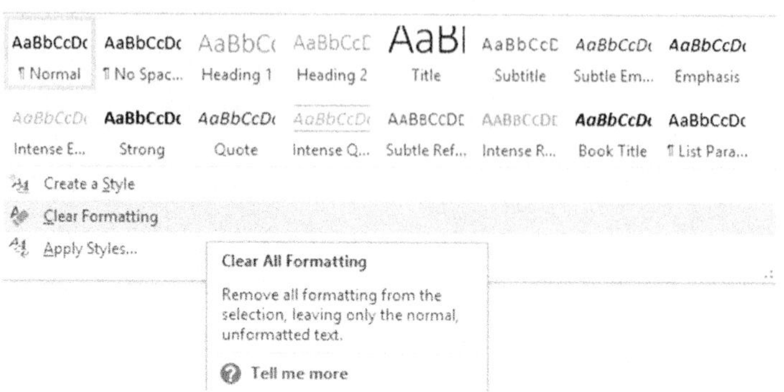

In most instances, this will indeed do what it says. If not try No. 2.

2 You can cut the offending text section out of your Word document and paste it into Notepad (Windows PC) or any other simple text editor. This strips out all underlying formatting. Then copy it out of the editing software and paste it back into Word. You will now be able to apply the style.

Miscellaneous Formatting Dos and Don'ts

Multiple line breaks or carriage returns

It is very tempting to insert one or more extra line breaks to move a following paragraph to the next page. This is bad typography and should be avoided; besides the fact that this will not translate into the eBook.

Instead, insert a page break before the line that is meant to be on the next page.

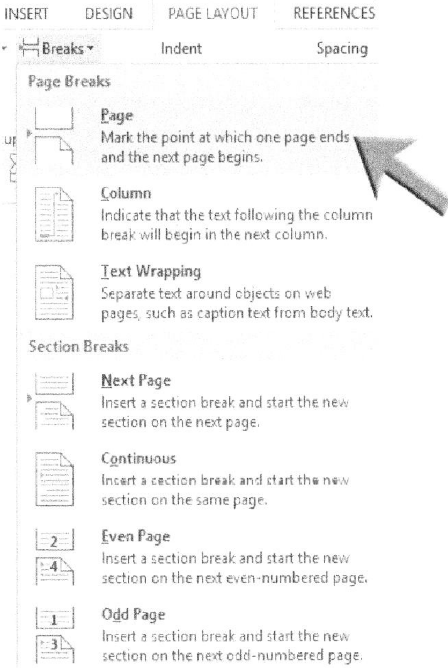

To insert a page break:

1. Click just before the text you wish to move to the next page.
2. Then click on the ‘Page Layout’ tab.
3. Then click on ‘Breaks’.
4. Finally, click on ‘Pagc’.

Applying <u>only to the print edition</u> of a book, extra line breaks may be inserted to move text elements down on a page. This would, for example, apply to a dedication that you would want to be in the middle of a page. Note, however, that when you do an eBook, any extra line breaks will first need to be removed.

Double or multiple spaces

It used to be considered good typography to use double spaces between sentences. This is no longer the case. In addition, should you use more than one space anywhere in your document, the extra spaces will all be removed when converting to an eBook format.

It is therefore good practice to avoid using double spaces. It is also a good idea to do a global find and replace for double spaces in a finished document.

- To search for a text element in Word you may use: CTRL+F
- To do a find and replace you may use CTRL+H

Additional eBook considerations

Just to add one more complication when moving on to an eBook: tables, charts, word-art and footnotes will not work.

The workaround for the **footnotes** is to incorporate them into the running text.

When it comes to the **tables, charts, word-art, etc.**, you can either find a way to reformat them and incorporate them in the regular running text, do without them, or convert them into images and place these into your document. The latter is often the best solution, as it will guarantee that what you see is what you will get.[11]

An example of this is the title page of this book. We wanted a particular layout that would not reflow during the eBook conversion. So, we created the look and feel we wanted and saved out an art file or image. This was then placed into the book document.

[11]. For help with creating an image see the section: Creating your own art file

Font (Typeface) selection

There are countless fonts; only a few of which you might ever wish to consider for the body copy of a book. There are fonts with and without a serif (the little bit that hangs off the end of the letter).

AaBbCc Sans-Serif font

AaBbCc Serif font

AaBbCc Serifs in Grey

It is considered good practice to use a minimal number of fonts in any given document; including books. One for the headlines and another for the body text usually works best. For example, the body copy of this book is *Bookman Old Style* – a serif font, while the headings are *Eras Demi* – a sans-serif font.

The choice of what fonts are used rests with the person designing the book – you!

Some fonts are more easily read. There are many artsy fonts that are not easily read, so take care to select a typeface that is pleasing to the eye and does not detract from the readability of the text.

Fonts of the same point size may not appear to be the same size. The individual letters may also be of significantly different width. This will, of course impact how much space the text uses, and thus influence the final page count.

The font size, measured in points,[12] also directly affects the page count of a given document. The larger the font size, the more space each character needs. Increasing the type size will increase the page count (and cost). On the other hand, making the type larger will also make the text easier to read. Conversely making the type size smaller will reduce the page count. It will also make it harder to read – particularly for older people.

Likewise, the greater the space between lines[13] the more pages a book will cover. Word allows the user to select multiples of line spacing or 'exactly', measured in points.

A good rule of thumb when typesetting text (body copy) is for the space between lines to be 2 points greater than the type size. The "Auto" or "Single" line spacing in most applications follows this rule of thumb. Any less and the text will appear crowded, more makes it look lighter.[14]

The space between paragraphs also has an influence on the page count.

Once again, taking this book as an example:

- The font size is 12pt
- The line spacing is single – it is 14pt
- The space before a paragraph is 3pt and after 6pt

---

[12] Type size is measured in points. There are 72 points (pt) to the inch, or 28.35 to the centimetre

[13] In a typesetting programme the line spacing is called leading. As with the font size it is measured in points.

[14] Note that for Manuscripts, book synopses and short story submissions, double line spacing is often specified.

Art fonts

Avoid using wingdings, dingbats, or other art fonts. The reason for this is that the individual characters of all (computer) fonts are described by the numeric ASCII code. ASCII stands for *American Standard Code for Information Interchange*. It's a 7-bit character code (7-digit Boolean number), where every number represents a unique character.

ASCII printable character codes are 32-127. They represent letters, digits, punctuation marks and a few miscellaneous symbols. This includes almost every character on your keyboard plus characters with accents etc.

The first 32 characters (codes 0-31) in the ASCII-table are unprintable control codes and are used to control peripherals such as printers. Codes 128-255 contain the extended characters. These include elements such as the euro, pound and other currency symbols, left and right quotation marks (as opposed to the straight quote marks) and many more.

Art fonts are fonts, where the letter of the alphabet is replaced with a symbol. This may look nice on the screen and may even print, but when converting to a digital eBook format the underlying ASCII information will be used and the symbol will revert to the corresponding letter.

If you find it necessary to use a particular symbol from an art font it is strongly recommended that you create an image and place this in your document. This is discussed in the chapter on 'Creating an image from a Word or Excel Document'.

Images

Image Placement

Most page layout programmes, including Word, allow the user to drag and drop images into the document. This is never best practice. It is always advisable to use the 'insert picture' feature.

In Word, click on the place where you would like to place the image, click on the 'insert' tab and then click on 'Pictures'. Then browse to where your photo is and click on 'insert'.

Linked Images

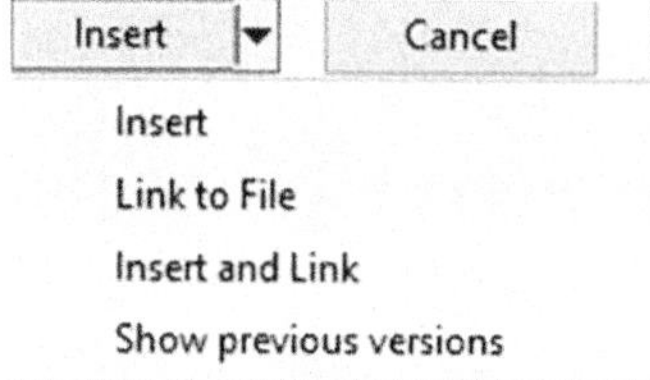

Newer versions of Word have a 'Link to file' option. This is available from the dropdown menu which is accessible by clicking on the down-arrow. Linking the image file in will automatically update the image should it be changed. You may 'Insert and Link' which places all the high res information in the word file, or just 'Link to File'.

'Link to File' is a very interesting option, as this only embeds the low-resolution screen representation in the Word document. This makes documents that are graphic intensive, such as this one, much smaller and less liable to crash.

Notes:

- If the images are linked in, then the relationship between the image folder and the Word document file must always stay the same otherwise the images will not print correctly.

- We had a problem with linked images when converting to Kindle by uploading the docx file to KDP. The linked images did not display.

Image Resolution

To print properly, images must be high resolution. If not, the printed image will look blurry or pixelated; not what was expected. (If you are only creating eBooks, this is not an issue.) Ideally this would be 300 dpi placed at 100%, or if the original image is screen resolution (72 dpi) placed at 25%. In a pinch, this can be reduced to about half this value, but not beyond that.

Follow the instructions below to ensure your images will remain high resolution, if your document will be printing on paper (as in a book) and you are placing images in it.

We have seen an anomaly with MS Word. If we place a high-resolution image (4"x5" @ 300 dpi) without altering its dimensions in Word, when we check the size, it shows the image as having been placed at 100%. However, if we change the resolution to 72 dpi in Photoshop, without resampling the image (this does not change the file size), the resulting image size is 16.7"x20.8". When this is then put in the document (appearing at the same size as above), Word "sees" it as having been placed at 24%. As both placed images are in fact precisely the same size, we ran this past the Amazon support team. They did not see it as an issue: As both placed images are of equal resolution, they should both print the same, as indeed they do. So, if in doubt, check the size of the original image.

If you have a document with high resolution placed images and you wish to email this to someone for review, then it might be advisable to create a second file in which you reduce the resolution of all the images in the document to "screen resolution" in order to significantly reduce the file size.

To do this click on any image in the document. In the menu bar at the top, click on "Picture Tools". This will change the options. To the left, click on "Compress Pictures."

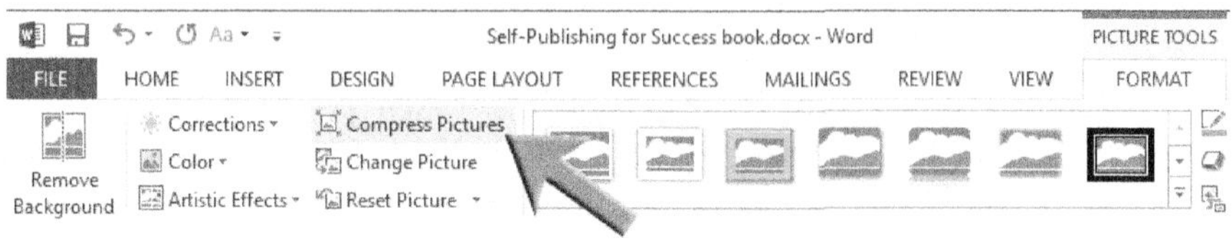

MS Word Picture Tools menu bar

In the resulting pop-up window, uncheck "Apply only to this image" and select "E-mail…", then hit OK.

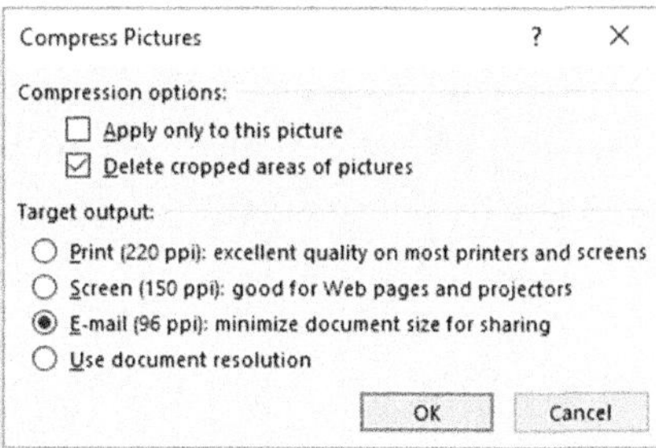

Just remember to save the file out with a different name, such as: *filename-lowres.docx*. If you do not, you may overwrite your original document.

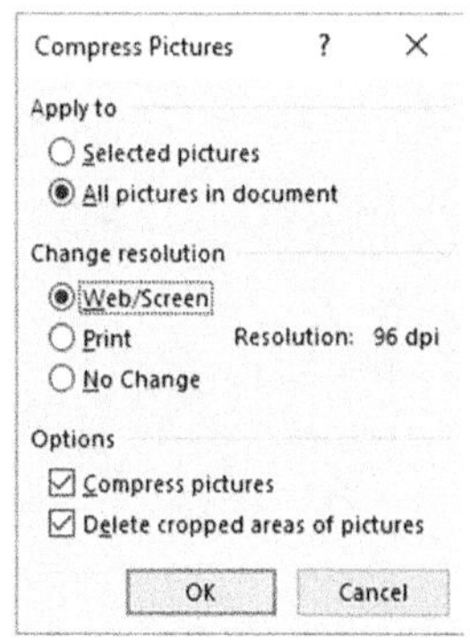

If you are working in an older version of Word or are in a workflow that requires the file to be saved out in an older version[15], then the second screen will look like this. Again, remember to save the file out with a different name, such as: *filename-lowres.doc.*

Ensure images are placed and saved as: High Resolution

Microsoft Word® has a very annoying default setting. When you place an image in your document, save the document and subsequently reopen it, the image appears to look fine. However, its resolution will automatically have been reduced to screen resolution – presumably to keep the file size down.

Of course, you do need to ensure that the images you place are indeed high resolution.

To get around this problem you must change the settings in Word before placing images into the document:

1. Under: File/Advanced Options:
2. Scroll down and select “Do not compress images in file”
3. Then select: “Apply to: All New Documents”

[15] You will come across this later on in the eBook chapter, where we discuss publishing your book using Smashwords.

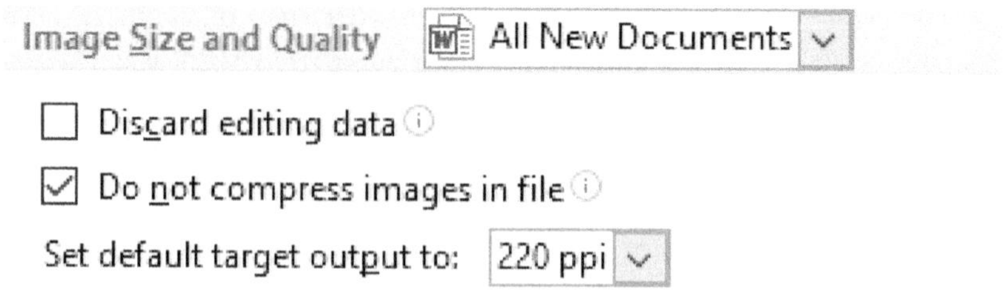

Image Size and Quality   All New Documents

☐ Discard editing data

☑ Do not compress images in file

Set default target output to: 220 ppi

It is a good idea to periodically check this setting as you continue to create new documents. On occasion we have seen it revert to the original default for some reason beyond our understanding.

True typesetting programmes, such as Adobe InDesign, QuarkXPress, PageMaker, or open source software such as Scribus get over this by placing the screen resolution image in the document and linking in its high-resolution original. These are then recombined when it comes time to print the file.

Image resolution is of particular interest when it comes to books with many pictures. Whereas the true typesetting programmes maintain a reasonable file size, the files produced in older versions of MS Word can become so huge that Word may crash frequently, potentially corrupting your document. The workaround we used here in the past, is to break up the document, print each part to pdf and then recombine in Acrobat Pro. Not ideal, but it does work. Newer versions of Word will allow images to be linked in. [16]

Adding art elements to your document

It is often desirable or even necessary to place an image or art element in your text in order to achieve a particular

---

[16] See note above on linked in images in Word

look or feel that will reproduce as expected in both print and eBook formats. Instances where this might be useful include:

- Title page
- Charts
- Word Art
- Graphs
- In-line graphic text elements
- Bugs or text separators

In all instances, think big. That means: recreate what you would like to place in your text as a graphic on a large page, such as A3 or tabloid – and or course, fill the page as best as you can. The reason for this is when the page is converted to a graphic it will be at screen resolution. However, when you then scale it down to work in your book, it will be high resolution and will print well, as the pixel count will not have been changed.[17]

The 'right' way to do this is to use a vector art programme such as Adobe Illustrator® or one of the Open Source alternatives such as Inkscape, Gravit or Vectr[18]. These all let you save the resulting file in .jpg, .gif or .png format, any of which you can place in your Word document.

If you are not comfortable using these programmes, you can create your image starting in MS Word or Excel. Use the latter for charts. This is explained below.

---

[17] See also the notes on image resolution.

[18] You will find suggestions for this on our book help webpage: whiteseahorse.ie/books

Bugs and other text art elements

A place you might wish to use a small art element such as an art font is as a 'bug' or text separator. These are often employed where there is a scene change within a chapter. These can be very simple, as in the following example, or quite elaborate.

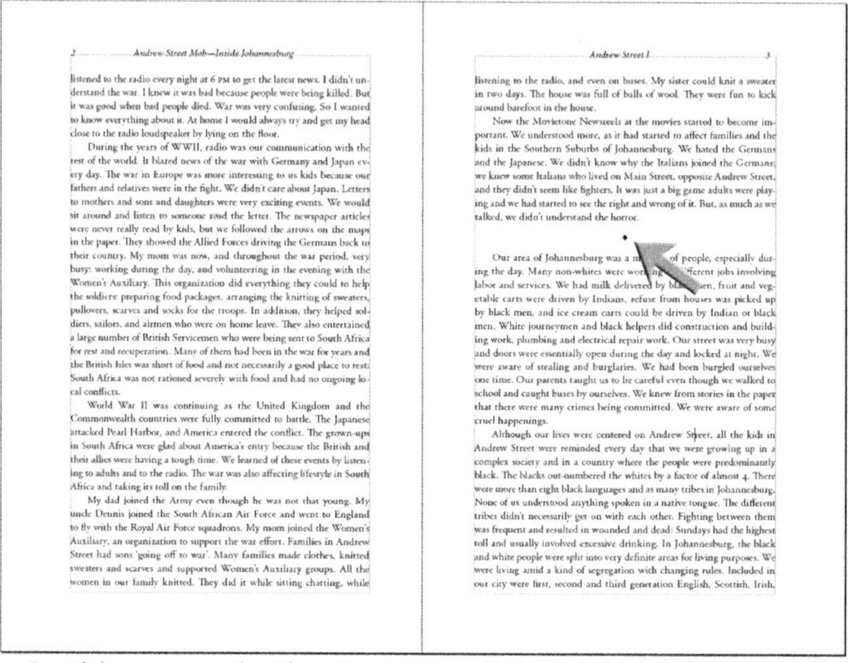

2 *Andrew Street Mob—Inside Johannesburg*

listened to the radio every night at 6 PM to get the latest news. I didn't understand the war. I knew it was bad because people were being killed. But it was good when bad people died. War was very confusing. So I wanted to know everything about it. At home I would always try and get my head close to the radio loudspeaker by lying on the floor.

During the years of WWII, radio was our communication with the rest of the world. It blared news of the war with Germany and Japan every day. The war in Europe was more interesting to us kids because our fathers and relatives were in the fight. We didn't care about Japan. Letters to mothers and sons and daughters were very exciting events. We would sit around and listen to someone read the letter. The newspaper articles were never really read by kids, but we followed the arrows on the maps in the paper. They showed the Allied Forces driving the Germans back to their country. My mom was now, and throughout the war period, very busy: working during the day, and volunteering in the evening with the Women's Auxiliary. This organization did everything they could to help the soldiers: preparing food packages, arranging the knitting of sweaters, pullovers, scarves and socks for the troops. In addition, they helped soldiers, sailors, and airmen who were on home leave. They also entertained a large number of British Servicemen who were being sent to South Africa for rest and recuperation. Many of them had been in the war for years and the British Isles was short of food and not necessarily a good place to rest: South Africa was not rationed severely with food and had no ongoing local conflicts.

World War II was continuing as the United Kingdom and the Commonwealth countries were fully committed to battle. The Japanese attacked Pearl Harbor, and America entered the conflict. The grown-ups in South Africa were glad about America's entry because the British and their allies were having a tough time. We learned of these events by listening to adults and to the radio. The war was also affecting lifestyle in South Africa and taking its toll on the family.

My dad joined the Army even though he was not that young. My uncle Dennis joined the South African Air Force and went to England to fly with the Royal Air Force squadrons. My mom joined the Women's Auxiliary, an organization to support the war effort. Families in Andrew Street had sons 'going off to war'. Many families made clothes, knitted sweaters and scarves and supported Women's Auxiliary groups. All the women in our family knitted. They did it while sitting chatting, while

Andrew Street I 3

listening to the radio, and even on buses. My sister could knit a sweater in two days. The house was full of balls of wool. They were fun to kick around barefoot in the house.

Now the Movietone Newsreels at the movies started to become important. We understood more, as it had started to affect families and the kids in the Southern Suburbs of Johannesburg. We hated the Germans and the Japanese. We didn't know why the Italians joined the Germans; we knew some Italians who lived on Main Street, opposite Andrew Street, and they didn't seem like fighters. It was just a big game adults were playing and we had started to see the right and wrong of it. But, as much as we talked, we didn't understand the horror.

•

Our area of Johannesburg was a m[illegible] of people, especially during the day. Many non-whites were wor[illegible]ng [illegible]fferent jobs involving labor and services. We had milk delivered by bl[illegible]en, fruit and vegetable carts were driven by Indians, refuse from houses was picked up by black men, and ice cream carts could be driven by Indian or black men. White journeymen and black helpers did construction and building work, plumbing and electrical repair work. Our street was very busy and doors were essentially open during the day and locked at night. We were aware of stealing and burglaries. We had been burgled ourselves one time. Our parents taught us to be careful even though we walked to school and caught buses by ourselves. We knew from stories in the paper that there were many crimes being committed. We were aware of some cruel happenings.

Although our lives were centered on Andrew Street, all the kids in Andrew Street were reminded every day that we were growing up in a complex society and in a country where the people were predominantly black. The blacks out-numbered the whites by a factor of almost 4. There were more than eight black languages and as many tribes in Johannesburg. None of us understood anything spoken in a native tongue. The different tribes didn't necessarily get on with each other. Fighting between them was frequent and resulted in wounded and dead: Sundays had the highest toll and usually involved excessive drinking. In Johannesburg, the black and white people were split into very definite areas for living purposes. We were living amid a kind of segregation with changing rules. Included in our city were first, second and third generation English, Scottish, Irish,

In this example the 'bug' is a big dot created with a lowercase 'l' in the font 'Wingdings'

Online art elements

If you search for 'text divider' or 'text separator' you will find a large volume of free and paid for such art elements. Example:

http://www.fontspace.com/category/dividers

Once downloaded you can place the file in your document crop to the piece you would like to use, and then resize to suit. You can even find some quite exotic art files.

An example of such a collection of suitable art elements is the following:

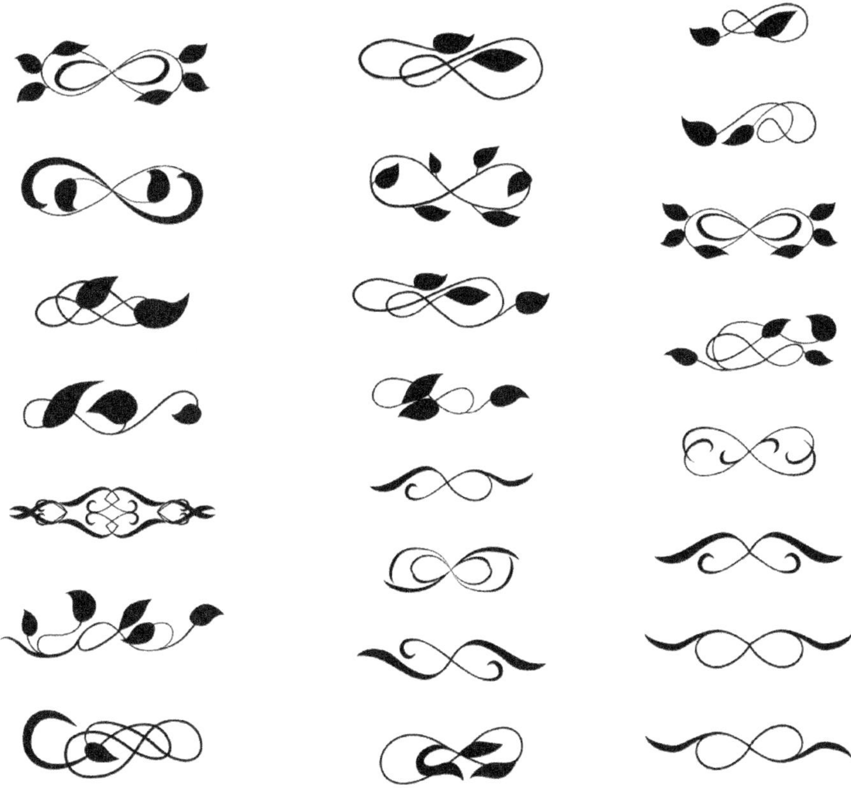

Any one of these images might make an attractive 'bug' for your manuscript. All you need to do is crop the image to the desired element, scale it to the desired size and then copy and paste to where needed.

Creating an art file from a Word or Excel document

If you want to create your own art element to use as a bug or if you have a chart, table, some Word art, or a title page you would like to create as an image and then place in your document, there are several workflows you may avail of. In any instance, the first step is to create the image you want as large as possible.

For a bug or text separator to be used in **Word**, you can go with a screen grab of a large image and then crop and reduce it as desired.

♋ – This is the Wingding version of the lowercase letter 'a'. It was placed in a Word doc, enlarged to the max, screen grabbed (Function + PRTSC), cropped, saved to this document's images folder (the result is a .png file). In this example it was placed in this document at 4%.

The other Word workflow for more complex art elements, such as a title page, chart, Word art, just a 'bug', etc., would be to create this on a larger (a4 or tabloid) page and save out as a .docx or .doc file or export as .pdf. The resulting file can then be converted to a .jpg image file using free online tools[19] and subsequently placed in your document.

For tables created in **Excel**, the workflow is similar:

1. Create and format your table as you would like to see it in print (make it large!), using all the tools available: Font, size, formatting, borders, shading, etc.
2. Under the page Layout tab
    a. Click on 'Size' and select a large page size, such as A3.
    b. Click on 'Orientation' for a horizontal of vertical layout.

---

[19] You will find suggestions for this on our book help webpage: whiteseahorse.ie/books

   c. Highlight all the cells of your table, including headlines etc.
   d. Click on 'Print Area' and select 'Set Print Area. This ensures that only the selected area will print.
3. Click on File, and then 'Export'. Then click on the button 'Create PDF' and name and place your file
   a. The pdf you created will open on your screen. If the table only fills a portion of the displayed page, enlarge the table in Excel starting with step 1.
4. You may now convert the .pdf file to a .jpg using free online tools[20] and then place the resulting file in your document.
   a. There are also online tools to directly convert an excel file to .jpg. However, following the above workflow will help ensure a maximum image size.

Cover Creation

"You can't tell a book by its cover." Well, whereas that may be true, the cover is the first thing anyone sees. It is what first catches their eye, whether they are looking for printed book or an eBook. So, the cover is indeed a very important part of your book. It needs to be given a lot of thought, designed effectively and set up correctly.

A fun exercise is to go to a bookstore and study the books on the shelves in the genre in which you are writing. Note which book catches your eye first. Note the colours of the books – which ones stand out? Is there a predominant

---

[20] You will find suggestions for this on our book help webpage: whiteseahorse.ie/books

colour? Note the titles and typefaces. Do all the books feature common elements on the cover? What does the spine show? How is the back cover handled?

Do the same online. Go to Amazon or Goodreads and look at all the books offered up to you in your category. Will yours stand out online?

Doing some market research will help you decide what might work for your book. It will also save you money when working with a book designer.

The more you think about what will make your book stand out and yet speak to the audience asking them to take it off the shelf, the better the cover designer can satisfy your interests. Saying something like, "I'll know what I like when I see it," is never helpful.

Design

If you are not a skilled and trained art director, cover design is certainly one area where professional input may be warranted. If you have no intention of selling your book and your only motive is to produce a gift for family or friends, then professional cover design is certainly optional.

If you do opt to design your own cover, the commonly used programmes include Adobe Photoshop, Adobe InDesign as well as freeware/open source programmes such as GIMP. All of these are feature rich but do require a good deal of learning in order to master the tools.

KDP also offers a very usable **online cover creator** tool, (see below for more information) which enables the user to design a very good, albeit basic cover.

Once you have a design you like, take it back to the book shop and see how it fits with the others already there.

Does it pop off the shelf? Ask people what they think. Most people love being asked for their opinion.

Title

When it comes to finding your book online or having someone take it down off the shelf in a bookstore, the title is a critical element. It may have come to you before or during the writing process, but it is something well worth reviewing again and again.

You should also do online searches for your title, in case someone has used the same one in the same genre. If this is the case, you really need to create an alternative.

Even if nobody has used your specific turn of phrase in the actual title, you may wish to add a sub-title. This can be more descriptive, giving the potential reader a bigger incentive to take your book off the shelf. The subtitle is more commonly used in the Americas than in Europe.

Back cover

The back cover is the place where you must convince the potential reader to open your book and start reading – in other words, to buy your book. Here you give away just enough of the plot of a novel, or a taste of the wisdom of a how-to book to unequivocally sway the purchasing decision.

The back cover "blurb" is also your "elevator speech." When someone asks you what your book is about, this is what you would recite between two floors of an elevator ride. It needs to be crisp and succinct, yet intriguing. You should be working on editing this to perfection from the moment your first draft is complete.

Crowd sourced opinions

If you are brave enough to put yourself "out there" and ask for the opinion of friends, family and acquaintances, you may do an online poll or comment posting.

We have done this on numerous occasions to find the right cover design, book title, or back cover copy. Each time we provide several versions and ask the simple question: "Which one of these would motivate you to take the book off a shelf or select it online and buy it?"

Each and every time it has been an amazing experience. Sometimes people have written long commentaries weighing the scenarios and perhaps combining elements of one with another. It caused us to redesign one cover completely with great results. With my first novel a viewer even noticed that I had used the wrong aircraft model in the cover illustration. Social media is a great free market research tool, especially for cover design. It pays to use it, just don't abuse it.

Cover Layout

Let us now take a look at the physical construction of a book cover. There are three areas that are of importance to the designer: **Front Cover, Back Cover and Spine**.

When designing a cover an understanding of how the cover is manufactured – printed, trimmed (cut) and folded – is important.

The book cover is printed on a larger sheet of thick paper. This then receives a layer of laminate to protect the artwork. It is then scored (or creased) along the fold lines, so that when the sheet is folded, it does not crack.

The next step is for the cover to be wrapped around and glued to the book block (stack of interior text pages). This then goes into a three-knife-trimmer, where the (also oversized) text pages and book cover are trimmed to the book's final size.

These are all mechanical processes. In any of these steps the book can quite literally bounce, so inaccuracies must be allowed for. One must consequently take into account that there needs to be a margin for error.

The designer must keep all important artwork, including the book title, logos, essential images and description a distance away from where it is intended that the paper is to be cut or trimmed, or where it is to be folded. The area for the artwork is called the "Live" area and is white on the following illustration. The background artwork must consequently also extend beyond the trim – it must "bleed" off the page.

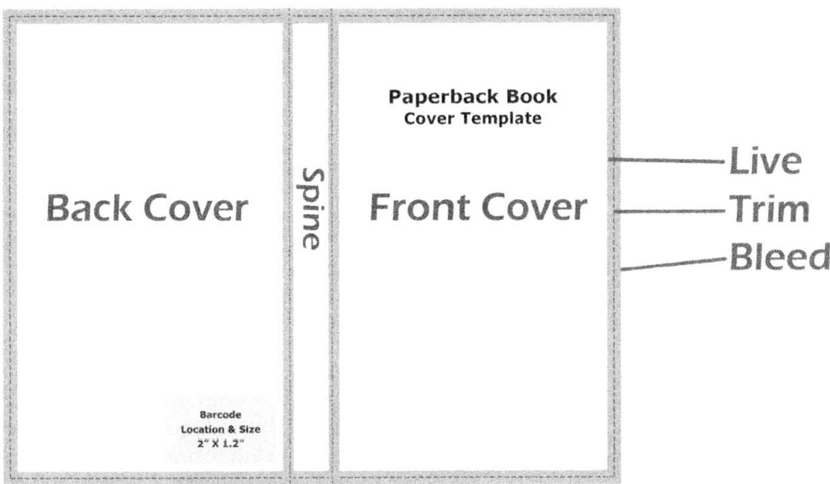

Specific to books (and most consumer packaging), there is also a rectangular area on the back cover reserved for the barcode.[21] It must remain devoid of "live", or important artwork. For publication through KDP, the position is fixed to the bottom right corner of the back cover.

Tip!

Download and use the provided template file

If you hire an artist to design your cover or do it yourself using an application such as Adobe Photoshop®, then you would be strongly advised to download and use the provided template. KDP and other self-publishing resources provide easy to use template files that are formatted to the dimensions, page count and type of paper to be used in your book. Their online cover creator incorporates this template.

The process is very simple and is based on the trim size, page count and paper type:

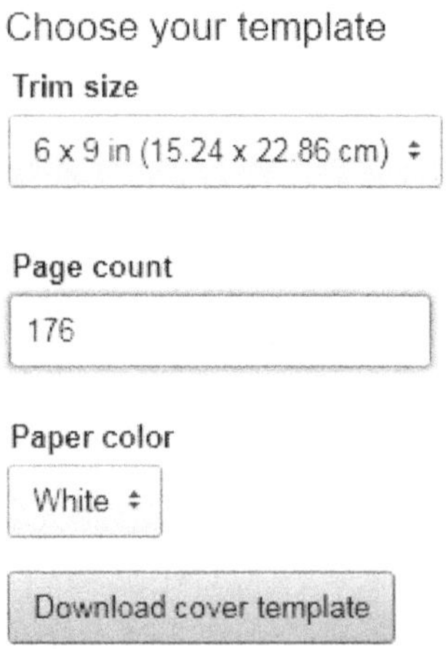

Choose your template
Trim size
6 x 9 in (15.24 x 22.86 cm)
Page count
176
Paper color
White
Download cover template

1. Select the trim size (dimensions) of your finished book.
2. Enter the final page count including any front or back matter.
3. Select the paper colour.

When you click on "Download cover template", you will receive a zip file containing a pdf and a .png file.

---

[21] On a book, this is the ISBN. The International Standard Book Number is something every book needs in order to be sold through online or bricks and mortar resellers. More on this in the Appendix.

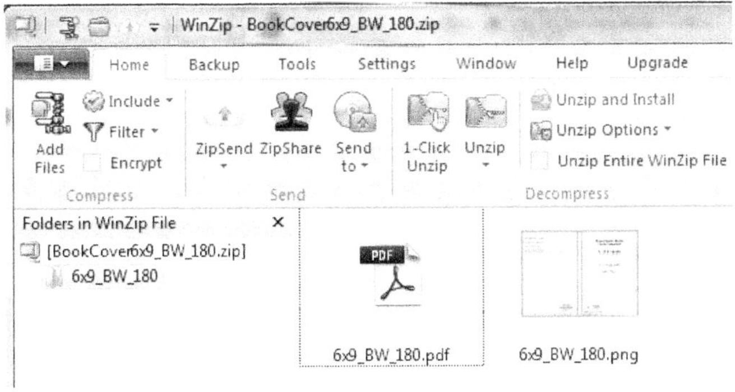

Of note is that the final document dimensions of the resulting cover file must be equal to the bleed size as determined by the template. If you do not set your cover document up to the correct bleed size, you will get unexpected results, as the production system is fully automated.

To use the provided template file, follow these steps:

1. Open the PDF or PNG file for the Paperback Book Cover Template in your image-editing software (Photoshop or GIMP).
2. The template will determine the dimensions of your cover document. Do not make the document larger than the template. This will lead to errors when you later upload the file to KDP[22].
3. Create a new layer in your image-editing software. This layer will serve as the design layer. Do not move the guide layer, as it is properly aligned for the KDP printing specifications.
4. Add guides to your document for the live, trim and bleed areas and also for the folds either side of the spine, as described earlier.

---

22 Other instructions as to document dimensions may apply if sending your cover file to a commercial or offline POD printer.

5. We also prefer to add additional guides ¼" or 75mm in from the trim for the text elements.
6. Hide or turn off the template layer.
7. Design your cover in the design layers (above the template layer), using the guides. The background artwork should extend to the outside edge of the bleed area (the template's pink zone) to ensure a white border will not appear within the printed work.
8. Ensure text and/or images that are intended to be read do not extend into the pink zones of the template. In fact, you may wish to keep them a further 3-5 mm or 1/8 inch in from that (1/4" from the trim – hence the additional guide lines).
9. The barcode area is indicated in yellow on the template. Do not place important images or text intending to be read in the barcode location.
10. Once your design is complete, you will need to turn off (hide) the guide layer. If you do not, it may be printed on your final product. Your cover may also be rejected during the review process. If you are unable to turn off the guide layer, then you will need to format the artwork so that it completely covers the guide layer.
1. When you have finished your cover design:
    a. Save your finished file.
    b. Ensure that the template layer is hidden.
    c. Flatten the layers.
    d. Save the file as a press quality PDF.
    e. This is the file you will upload to KDP.

Other cover images

You will also want to have cover image files for other uses such as your marketing efforts. Continue on from the above as follows:

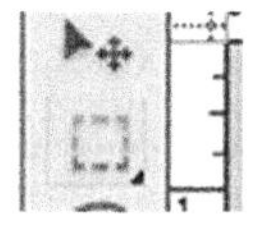

1. Using the Rectangular Marquee tool follow the trim line. And then crop the image.
2. Save this out as a JPEG file.
3. Using the Marquee tool again select the front cover and crop the image.
4. Save the result out as a JPEG, giving it a different name, such as *MyCoverFile-FC.jpg*
5. If you need lower resolution versions of this file for other purposes, such as for your web page, you may do this now and save each one out with an appropriate name.

Ordering Your Own Books

Short run book printing and Print on Demand are not mutually exclusive to the self-published author. There is a role for each, which optimizes your return while limiting your costs. Here are some reasons you may wish to order copies of your book:

- You may order single copies:
  - For you, your family or your friends
  - Review copies (worldwide direct shipping)
- You may order multiple copies
  - Review copies (to send out yourself to critics for review)
  - For a book launch
  - Lectures/speaking engagements (Book signings)
- You may order larger quantities
  - Working with a distributor
  - Direct sale after speaking engagements

You can avail of three principal options when printing your own books.

- Single copies (POD): 1 - 50 copies
- Short run book printing: 50 - 1,000 copies
- Longer run book printing: 1000+ copies

As each of these workflows relies on different types of technology, they all have different production cost considerations. Of primary interest to the author is the delivered cost per copy. In each instance this cost has three contributing factors:

- Preparation
- Production
- Shipping

As quantities increase, longer run length technologies have a lower cost per unit. Where this happens is what is called a cross-over point.

Based on the page count, type of paper, trim size, and finishing, each book has different cost factors associated with it. Different suppliers may also not have the same cost basis in their respective workflows.

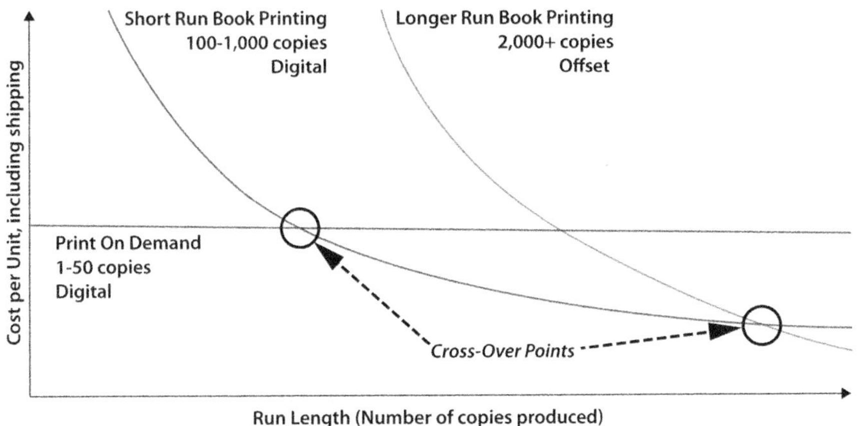

Print On Demand

POD is almost fully automated, and the production is entirely digital. The only contributing costs are the manufacture of the book and its shipping costs. The cost per copy is thus fairly constant, irrespective of how many copies are ordered. There is a small savings as quantities increase due only to the reduced cost of shipping.

There are also local (offline) POD options. In this instance there may be an initial setup cost to cover manually reviewing and queuing up the files for printing. After this, the cost per unit us usually quite constant as well. Where this is available, the advantage is the super-short turnaround time.

Short Run Printing

Like POD, short run book printing is entirely digital. However, there is a certain amount of work in preparing files and equipment for short run book printing. Files are manually reviewed and queued up for printing. Cutting and bindery equipment is adjusted and manually set up for each subsequent job.

Each print run is unique and as there is little automation, the cost for this preparation work is front loaded into each job. Shorter run lengths thus have initially higher costs per unit, but as the quantity of books increases, each book produced costs less, until a point is reached where this is less than the POD cost.

Longer Run Printing

Likewise, setting up a longer print run of books is even more costly. The production method here is offset printing technology, using printing plates and ink on paper. The only digital component is in the production of the plates. After that, it is all conventional printing.

Getting a job running on a printing press is costly. The bindery, as with the short run printing, is manually set up, which also adds to the up-front costs. However, once the presses are rolling, they can keep rolling for a long time at a relatively low cost. The more books produced, the lower the cost per unit, until this cost curve dips below that of the digital short run printing.

Selling Your Book Online with KDP

KDP[23] is a customizable POD self-publishing service that helps you publish your book the way you envision it. See: kdp.amazon.com

KDP allows you to publish your book your way, at zero cost, with no pressure to buy services you don't want or that don't help your process. The KDP team is available to answer questions throughout the procedure, either via email or phone.

There Is *No* Hassle

You will not be contacted by KDP sales people trying to sell you services or bind you in with a contract.[24] Unless you opt to avail of the paid-for services or have a specific question you will not be bothered.

There Is *No* Cost

An important thing to remember is that if you are willing and able to do everything yourself (type, design, layout, etc.), getting your book published will cost you absolutely nothing. There are also no commitments or obligations.

This is of particular interest to those who wish to publish a memoir, family history, children's book, or whatever, without the desire or need to ever sell a single copy. You

---

[23] See note in the front matter. There are other service providers (see appendix) that may or may not provide equal or better services. Kindle Direct Publishing (KDP) is an Amazon company. We do not derive any benefit whatsoever from KDP or Amazon or its affiliates for using them as an example. Our printed titles are published through KDP and this book and this section is based on our own personal experience.

[24] We have experienced this with other providers.

do not need to publish your title on Amazon. You may by all means upload and process your book and then just order one copy for yourself, or perhaps 5 copies for your family and friends. KDP makes a small amount of money on every book printed and shipped out. They do not care how many copies of your book are produced.

Of course, if you are an EL James and sell hundreds of thousands of copies of your title through KDP, they make out like bandits, laughing all the way to the bank – and, by the way, so do you; as did she!

Is help available?

If you feel you need broad assistance, KDP has many helpful documents to guide you along.

The KDP website also has some excellent free tools. For example, you can instantly calculate what your royalties would be under different pricing scenarios, through different sales channels. There are also free templates to help you create a professional looking book.

To save you the hassle of finding this information, we have published links to of these at:

www.whiteseahorse.ie/books

Setting up Your KDP Account

Setting up an account with KDP is quick and easy. The initial information they need is a username (your email address) and a password; remember to use a unique combination and to make a note of it for future reference.

Once in, there are three headings you need to provide information for:

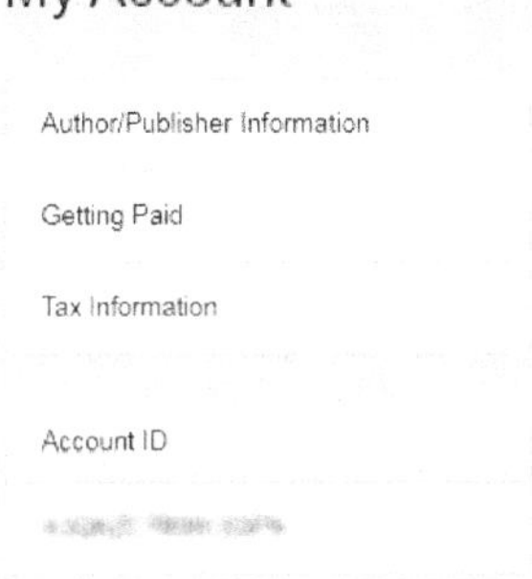

The importance of each of these is fairly straightforward. If you are wishing to sell books online, then particular care should be given to the **Getting Paid** heading. If at any time you are uncertain as to what is needed, click on “save” to preserve what you have done and take the time to research the best answer.

Your Amazon account information is also important, as this is how you will be charged for any purchases you make from KDP/Amazon.

Adding a Title to KDP - A Step by Step Guide

There are several items of information you might want to have at hand before you start the process of adding a new title. We like to collect this information in one or more text documents that we save into the book’s job folder. This is not required, but will speed things up for you (more on these below):

- Title
- Author
- Series
- Publication date

- ISBN (if you already have one, otherwise KDP will provide this)
- Description
- Author biography
- Category
- Keywords

The following is a step-by step description of the process that builds on the chapter on "Creating your Book". (The services offered by KDP and the details of the individual screen grabs shown will change from time to time.) KDP allows you to save your work at any point, so there is no need to rush through and perhaps miss something.

You may also change things as you go along. The exceptions to this are the ISBN, which cannot be changed once it has been assigned and the book title information, which cannot be changed once the title has been submitted for review. All the rest may be changed at any time in the future but may require that the book is reviewed again before re-release.

If you do wish to change the title, by all means start over and then delete the old version. There is no charge for this.

Your Bookshelf

Your Bookshelf is your home page on KDP. It will look similar to the following image. Here you will find a list of all your titles.

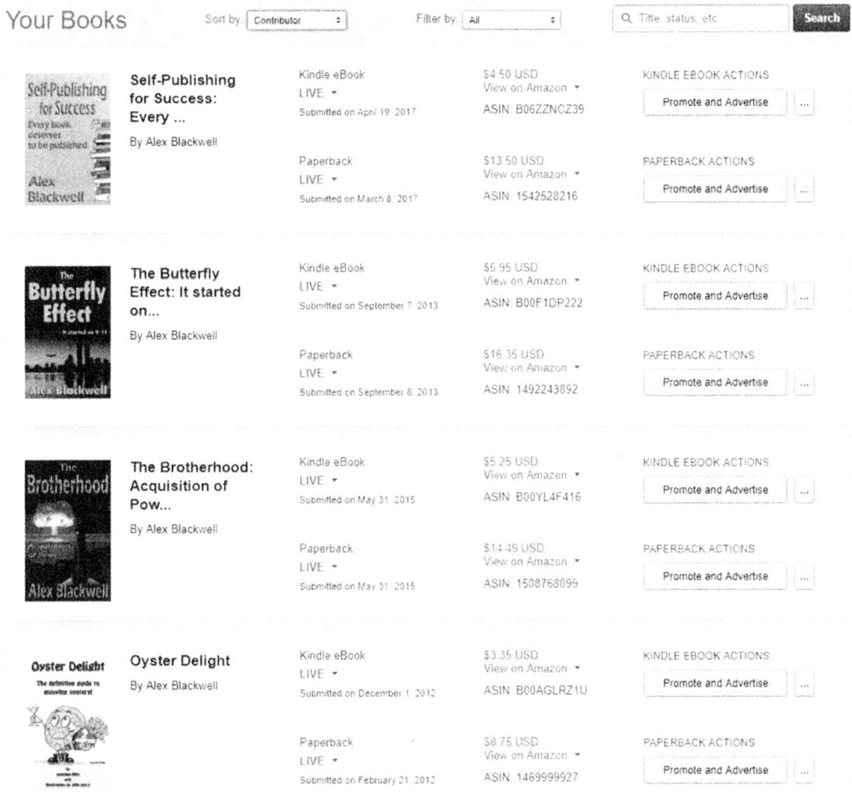

This is also where you will be able to view and download reports, including your annual sales.

Adding a new paperback book title

Once you have set up your account, adding a new title is quite straight forward. The process is entirely menu driven and there is helpful information along the way.

To add a new title, you just click on "Paperback" under the "Create a New Title" heading at the top of your bookshelf page. Note that you may also start the process for your Kindle eBook here.

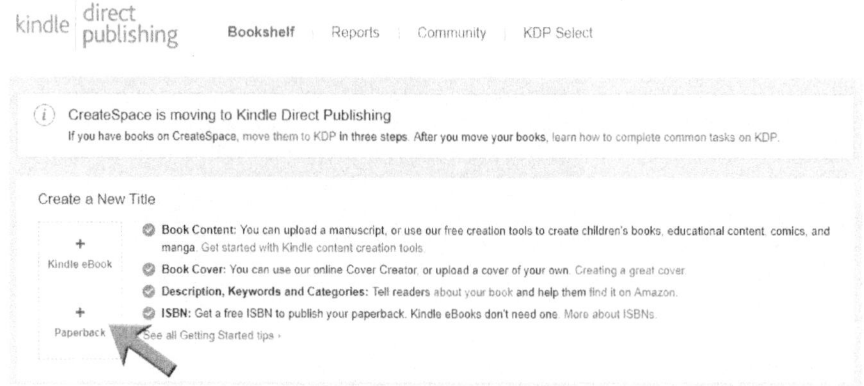

Paperback Details Page

This brings you to the Paperback Details Page. Here will select or enter all the information about your book.

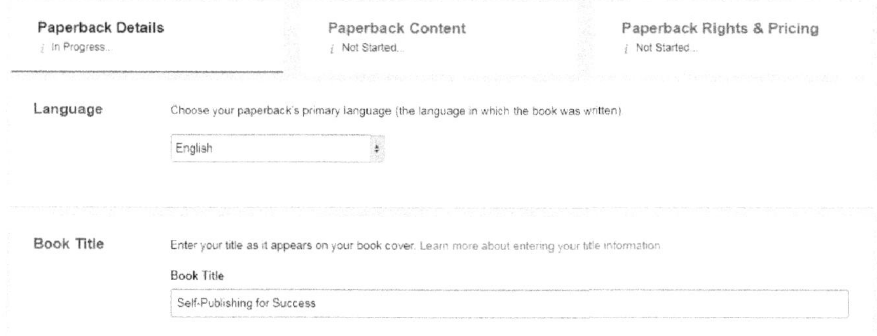

Notes:

- You may click on "Save as Draft" at any point in the process to save your work and do something else.
- Next to most items you will find a link. Clicking on this will provide some helpful information on what the item is intended for.

Language

From the drop-down menu select the language the book is written in. The default is English.

Book Title

Enter the book's title and sub-title if appropriate. As mentioned earlier, the title is very important. Research this thoroughly before continuing. If there are other similar titles, or if your book needs more description to differentiate it from other titles, then select a sub-title as well.

Series

Is the book part of a series? If so, is it the first? For example, we have set up "White Seahorse Classics" as an imprint. We use the Series Title to group them together on Amazon, as this appears as part of the title. In this case, we do not use a volume number.

Edition Number

If this is a title you have previously published, and this is an updated or revised edition, you may indicate this here also. A numeric entry is called for here.

Author

Here you enter the name of the primary author. This can be an actual name or a pen name. It is under this name that the book will be sorted on Amazon.

Contributors

You may also add any number of co-authors, editors, illustrators and other optional contributors.

Description

"Description" is an important element where a good bit of wordsmithing is called for. This is a **description** of your title (max 4,000 characters, including spaces.) This is what people will see on Amazon. It is what they will base their purchasing decision on.

If space allows, you might add an **author biography**. This is your opportunity to introduce yourself and to state what makes you interesting, or your book worth reading.

Publishing Rights

Is this your own work, or are you reproducing a book from the public domain (out of copyright)? Our own Classics imprint falls under the public domain category.

Keywords

The **keywords** are essential to help people find your book. You may enter up to five keywords separated by a comma and a space. Your book title and your author name are separate from this, so do not repeat them. Try to avoid using terms such as: novel, or thriller. Instead use terms that actually key into the content of what you have written. These keywords will be added to your book's Amazon listing page as embedded meta tags. These are important and are how someone may find your book when searching on Amazon. The keywords are also catalogued by search engines like Google. This is how potential readers may find your book.

Categories

Think of Categories as sections in a book shop.

The Categories listed here are the Book Industry Standards and Communications (**BISAC**) categories are used by the book-selling industry to help identify and group books by their subject matter. Browse through the options and select two that work best for your book. If possible, try to avoid the catchalls such as "fiction/thriller". Wherever you can, it is best to stand out. Alternatively, if you know it, you may also enter the appropriate BISAC code.

Adult Content

If your book contains language, situations, or images inappropriate for children under 18 years of age, then you will select 'yes' under "Adult Content", otherwise leave it at the default of 'no'.

Once you have completed this simple form, you can click "Save as Draft", if you wish to do something else. Alternatively, you can click on "Save & Continue".

Paperback Content

The Paperback Content page has further selections for you to make.

Print ISBN

The **International Standard Book Number (ISBN)** is something every book need to be sold through online or bricks and mortar resellers. By and large, the ISBN is used globally as a title's catalogue number.

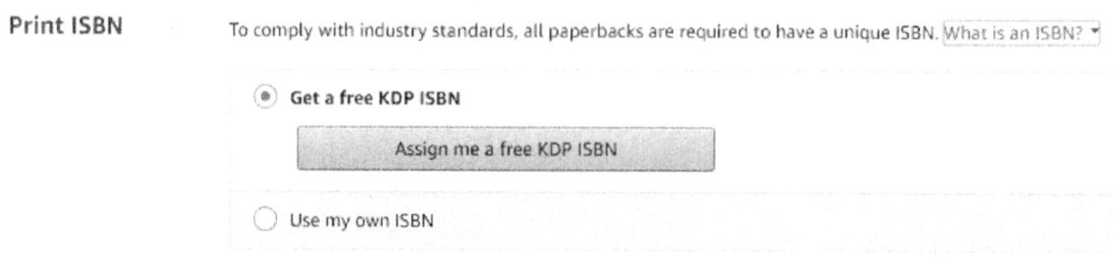

Your choices are to use your own ISBN, or to have KDP provide one for you.[25] Any person may obtain their own ISBN – at a cost. As part of their service, KDP provides this for free.

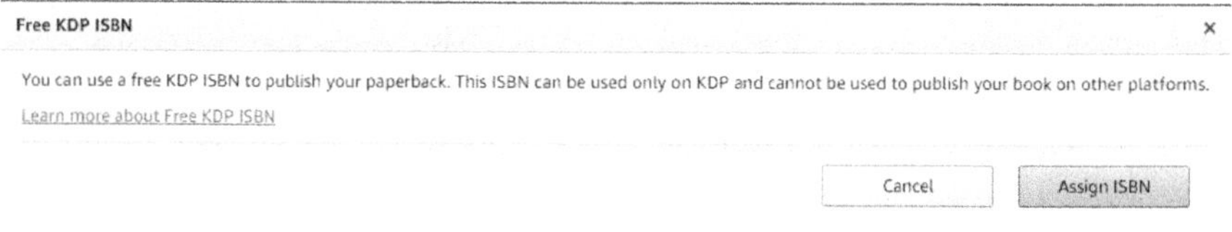

What one must consider is that the owner of the ISBN is the **"publisher of record"**. In my printing company, we used to provide these numbers to our customers. We were thus their publisher of record. Similarly, if you avail of the free ISBN from KDP, they will be the publisher of record, though you still retain the copyright and remain the author. As obtaining a number involves some work and cost, we (White Seahorse Publishing) use KDP assigned ISBN numbers for all our printed book titles.

Once KDP assigns an ISBN, it cannot be changed. Of note is that you may only use this ISBN when selling

[25] Your book's KDP ISBN information will be registered with BooksInPrint.com®

through KDP[26]. If you later go with another publisher, you will need a new ISBN.

There are two places the ISBN needs to be put in your book once it has been assigned:

- On the back cover in barcode format
    - KDP does this automatically for you
- In the front matter in numerical format

For more information on ISBN, please see the appendix.

Publication Date

Your publication date is the date on which your book was first published. The publication date is optional. You may put in a date of your choosing, as long as it is not in the past. You cannot change it after publishing your title. If you leave this blank, KDP will automatically use the date on which your book goes live (i.e. it is available for sale) on Amazon.

Print Options

If your book is already designed and laid out, this is where you select:

- Paper colour (white or cream – cream is slightly thicker)
- Black ink only or colour
- The trim size
- Whether there is bleed

---

[26] If you later order a quantity of books for yourself or for resale from KDP, they will come with their ISBN printed on the cover. If you order books from a different source, you should not use the KDP ISBN.

- The cover finish: gloss or matte laminate

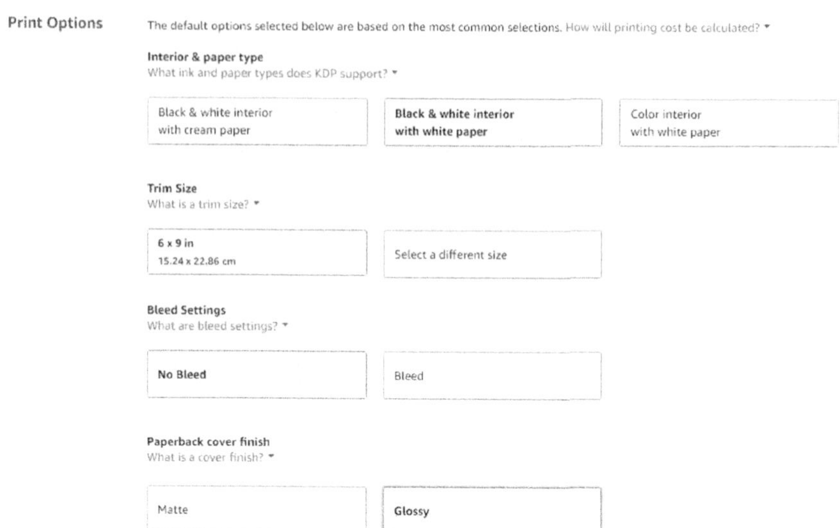

Printing cost varies depending on page count, paper type and ink type (black ink or colour ink). Trim size, bleed settings & cover finish don't affect printing cost.

6x9 inches is the most common size. "Bleed" is where an image may extend off the page or into the gutter.

The book covers are laminated. You have a choice of gloss or matte finish. For some books the matte finish looks very nice. For most the gloss is preferable. It makes the colours really stand out.

Manuscript

It is under the Manuscript heading that you will be able to upload the formatted interior of your book (manuscript).

Manuscript

Upload a manuscript of your book interior content. For best results, we recommend using a formatted PDF file to create your paperback. You can also upload a DOC (.doc), DOCX (.docx), HTML (.html), or RTF (.rtf). Learn more about manuscripts or download a KDP template for your preferred trim size.

Upload paperback manuscript

For best results, it is recommended to use a formatted PDF file to create your paperback. You can also upload a .doc, .docx, .html, or .rtf.

To help you along, KDP offers:

- MS Word templates in a variety of trim sizes[27]
- A step-by-step guide for formatting in Word
- On-demand webinars with best practices and tips

If your book has not yet been laid out, preformatted MS Word template files are available for download from this page under the Manuscript heading. These come as blank documents or with sample text. The latter include formatted front matter (e.g., title page, table of contents) and chapters with placeholder text. You'll customize the parts you want to keep and delete the sections you don't. The files we have provided include provision of additional front matter sections as well as additional formatting. You will find these at: www.whiteseahorse.ie/books

In either case they allow you to copy and paste in your text.

---

[27] Template files are also available at: www.whiteseahorse.ie/books

Book Cover

Here you have the choice between launching the KDP Cover Creator or uploading your finished cover.

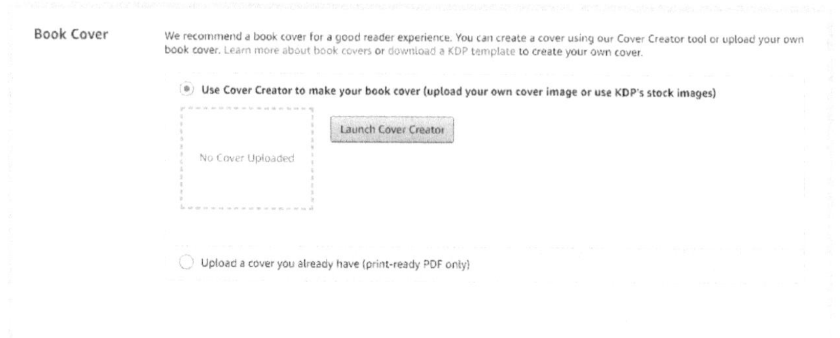
Book Cover
We recommend a book cover for a good reader experience. You can create a cover using our Cover Creator tool or upload your own book cover. Learn more about book covers or download a KDP template to create your own cover.
Use Cover Creator to make your book cover (upload your own cover image or use KDP's stock images)
Launch Cover Creator
No Cover Uploaded
Upload a cover you already have (print-ready PDF only)

KDP Cover Creator

KDP provides a free **Cover Creator** tool that helps you design a basic, but professional-quality eBook or paperback book cover using your own photos, logos and text. The tool allows you to customize your cover with a variety of provided layout templates and fonts. Cover Creator uses the book details you entered during title setup (see Adding a Title to KDP) This tool automatically formats and sizes your cover based on your book's trim size, paper type and page count. It adds your book's ISBN to the barcode area of the back cover. Many of the provided templates allow you to choose an image from their image gallery or upload your own image. The tool accepts JPG, PNG and GIF files.

Tip!

A recommended use of the Cover Creator would be to create a temporary cover if you are sending your manuscript out to proof readers or editors. While they are reviewing your book, you can take your time creating the perfect cover.

Using Cover Creator

Go to your Bookshelf (You will already have added your title to KDP) and find the book you want to create a cover for.

Next to either the Paperback Actions or Kindle eBook Actions menus, hold your mouse over the ellipsis button ("..."). Choose 'Edit Paperback' content or 'Edit eBook' content. (you have already completed the book details page.) You may have to sign in again at this point. Scroll down to Book cover. Click "Launch Cover Creator". A window will appear explaining the three steps: 'choose design', 'style & edit', 'preview'. Click on: Continue.

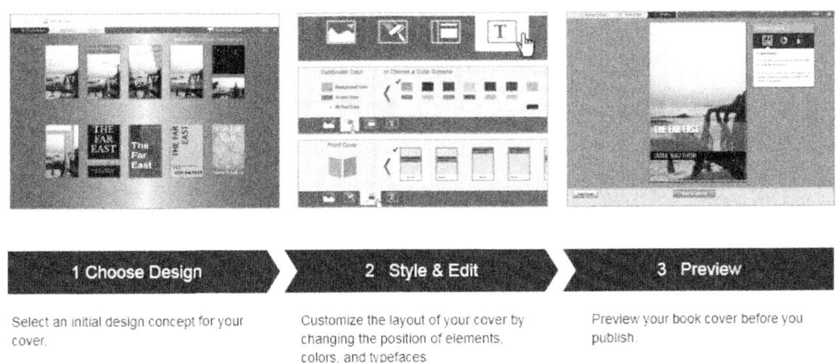

THE FAR EAST
1 Choose Design
Select an initial design concept for your cover.
2 Style & Edit
Customize the layout of your cover by changing the position of elements, colors, and typefaces
3 Preview
Preview your book cover before you publish.

Choose a stock image from their gallery or upload your own image. If you use your own image, make sure you own the rights to it and that it's high resolution. You may also download stock photography for this. There are countless free and paid-for online resources. See our web page for suggestions: whiteseahorse.ie/books

Image resolution is measured in dots or pixels per inch (dpi or ppi). Images with a high dpi (300 or higher) will be crisper than those with low dpi (less than 300) at full size. If your image is of a too low resolution a little warning triangle will appear when you upload. Mouse over this and you will see what the problem is.

After adding your image or selecting one of theirs, choose your design. When choosing, think about how the layout works for your image.

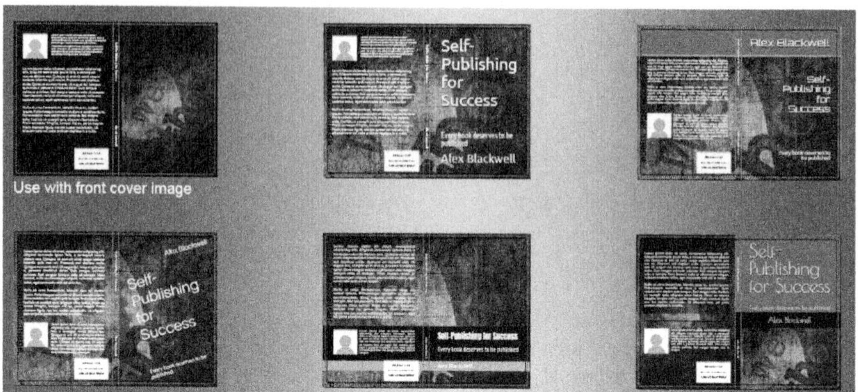

Choose your colour scheme, layout, and font. When making your selection, think about how these elements reflect the content of your book. Make sure the cover text doesn't blend into the background. This often happens because the text and background colour are too similar. Your cover text should also be large and clear enough.

You may change or replace your cover image

Click anywhere on the cover where there are no other elements such as text boxes. The dialog box "Edit cover image" will appear with options to choose a new image or change the current image's size, position, and rotation.

If you're publishing a paperback, add your book description, optional author biography, and optional author photo to the back cover. This is where you must entice a potential reader to buy your book.

Preview your cover. If you are satisfied, click Save & submit at the bottom of the screen.

Uploading your own cover design

Assuming you have designed your own cover as described in the chapter on Cover Creation, you may select “Upload a cover...” instead of working with the Cover Creator.

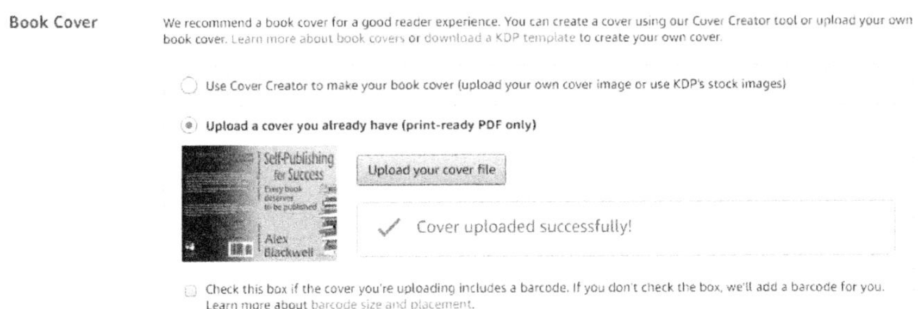

Book Cover
We recommend a book cover for a good reader experience. You can create a cover using our Cover Creator tool or upload your own book cover. Learn more about book covers or download a KDP template to create your own cover.
Use Cover Creator to make your book cover (upload your own cover image or use KDP's stock images)
Upload a cover you already have (print-ready PDF only)
Self-Publishing for Success
Alex Blackwell
Upload your cover file
Cover uploaded successfully!
Check this box if the cover you're uploading includes a barcode. If you don't check the box, we'll add a barcode for you.
Learn more about barcode size and placement.

Book Preview

Once the manuscript and cover are uploaded, they are checked for quality issues. These may include low resolution images, text too close to the edge of the page, etc.

Checking your cover for quality issues...

KDP is processing your manuscript and book cover to generate a print-ready file.
This requires a number of steps and can take several minutes.

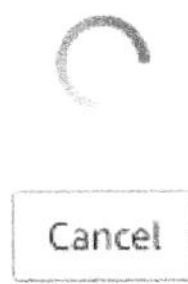

When your manuscript and cover files are approved, a process that is quite fast, it is time to review your book.

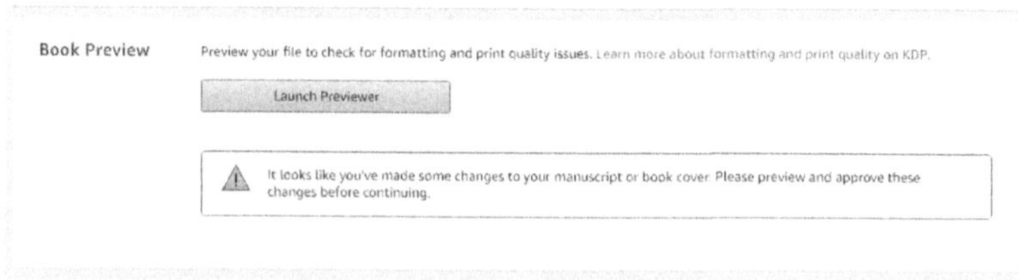

After clicking on the “Launch Preview” button the files will be processed, and the digital view launched.

The cover is always printed in colour and will appear with the back cover, spine and front cover. Check everything to see if it works the way you intended.

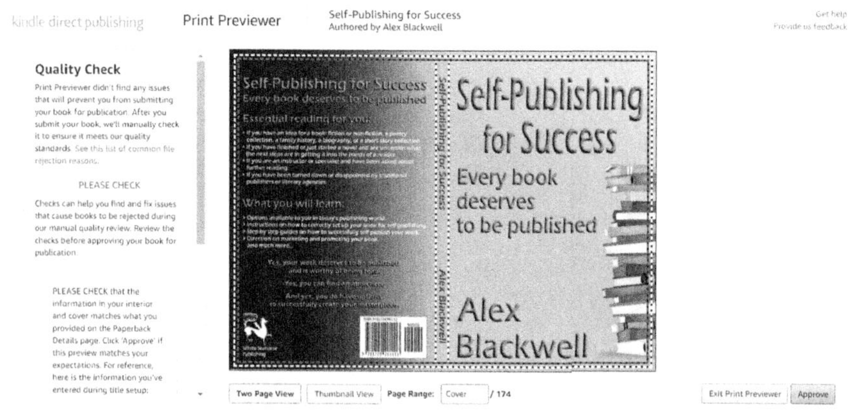

As you mouse over the outer edge of the right-hand page an arrow will pop up. Click on this to advance to the next pages.

Note that if you have placed colour images in the manuscript and are printing the book in Black and White, they will appear in colour at this stage. By all means leave them in colour, as this will be good if/when you do your eBook.

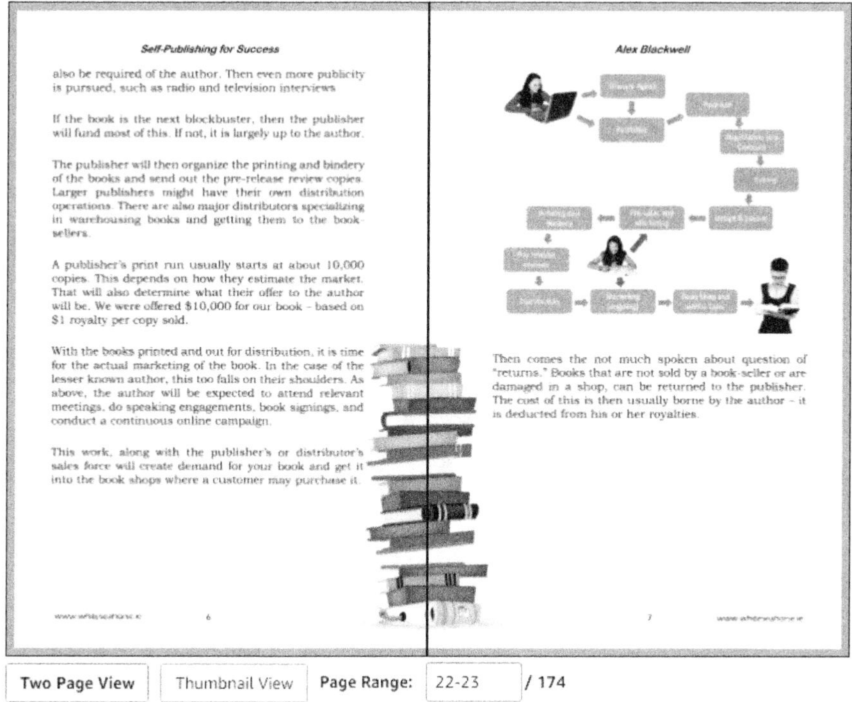

Self-Publishing for Success

also be required of the author. Then even more publicity is pursued, such as radio and television interviews

If the book is the next blockbuster, then the publisher will fund most of this. If not, it is largely up to the author.

The publisher will then organize the printing and bindery of the books and send out the pre-release review copies. Larger publishers might have their own distribution operations. There are also major distributors specializing in warehousing books and getting them to the book-sellers.

A publisher's print run usually starts at about 10,000 copies. This depends on how they estimate the market. That will also determine what their offer to the author will be. We were offered $10,000 for our book - based on $1 royalty per copy sold.

With the books printed and out for distribution, it is time for the actual marketing of the book. In the case of the lesser known author, this too falls on their shoulders. As above, the author will be expected to attend relevant meetings, do speaking engagements, book signings, and conduct a continuous online campaign.

This work, along with the publisher's or distributor's sales force will create demand for your book and get it into the book shops where a customer may purchase it.

6

Alex Blackwell

Then comes the not much spoken about question of "returns." Books that are not sold by a book-seller or are damaged in a shop, can be returned to the publisher. The cost of this is then usually borne by the author - it is deducted from his or her royalties.

7

If you would like to take a break and do something else, you may click on "Exit Print Previewer" at any time. Once you have reviewed your entire book and are happy with the way it looks, click on "Approve".

Paperback Rights and Pricing: Setting your book up for online sales

Provided you intend to allow people to purchase copies of your book, you will want to review and complete this page.

At the bottom of this page you will find a link to order a proof copy of your book. This is something we always advise doing, as it is your opportunity of holding your printed book in your hands and seeing how it looks and works. It is also how you will be able to do a final proofreading of your book. It is almost guaranteed that you will find typographical errors in the printed proof.

If you just want to produce a limited number of copies of your book, you will still need to complete this page so that you will be able to order author copies through Amazon – if you do not tell anyone about the book it is quite unlikely that anyone will find it. You can always un-publish it once you have ordered your copies if you want to keep it secret.

Territories

If you have written your book and not sold any territorial rights to it to another party, you retain the worldwide rights to your book.

Pricing & Royalty

First, select your **Primary Marketplace**. This is the Amazon marketplace where you expect the majority of your book sales. You can use the price set for this marketplace as a base to automatically convert prices into local currency for other marketplaces where your book will be sold.

Your **Royalty** is 60% of the sale price, less the calculated printing cost for all Amazon market places. Amazon calculates suggested list pricing for their other market places. You may accept this as is. At your discretion, you may also adjust the pricing for these outlets.

Where **VAT** is applicable, Amazon will add this on and pay it to the tax collector in the relevant jurisdiction. Although you therefore have no obligation to pay VAT on the sales of your books, you still have to report these sales if you are VAT registered. You also need to report the sales as income at year end.

Amazon calculates a **Minimum List Price** based on your book's printing cost. This ensures that your royalties are always enough to cover the cost to print your book.

By checking '**Expanded Distribution**', your book will be made available through bookstores, online retailers, libraries, and academic institutions.

With one of our non-fiction books we regularly see Expanded Distribution purchases of five or ten copies. These are copies that would otherwise not have made it out to the public. Granted that we make very little money on these sales, but we also have no out of pocket costs. The result is thus a net profit, a greater level of exposure, a higher sales ranking and hopefully more future sales.

Amazon Associates

Amazon has an "Associates Programme" you may enrol in. Here you earn a small percentage of each sale Amazon makes to someone who has clicked on your link on your website. This also applies to purchases of your own book. It is therefore well worth your while to set up Amazon Associates accounts (US and Europe) and push the sales from Amazon through their provided widgets or links. Every sale of the above-mentioned non-fiction book that goes through our associate's link earns us an additional 37 cents "**advertising fees**" – money that would otherwise have been left on the table – or in Amazon's pocket.

We have also found that these customers often go on to make other purchases on Amazon in the same online session – sometimes for very expensive items, netting us several additional dollars.

Getting your book printed locally or with a commercial book printer

Using your designed cover with a book printer

The pdf of your cover can be used as is with most commercial printers. You do not have to leave a white space for the ISBN. If you have your own ISBN, you may use it in place of the one provided by KDP.

If printing locally on equipment like the **Espresso Book Machine (EBM)**, a different page size may be required for your cover. For the EBM, the artwork needs to be centred on an A3 sheet. In this case increase your canvas size in Photoshop to 420 x 297mm and save the resulting artwork out as a pdf as per the above instructions.

Using your text pages with a book printer

If your text pages were correctly formatted for KDP, the pdf file you created will work just fine. As above either replace the ISBN number in the front matter with your own number, or leave this blank.

Digital or eBooks

Knowing that about half of the people reading books like to read a digital book (including those who also read print books), creating an eBook is an important part of self-publishing. As mentioned earlier, all our books are available in print and digital formats, as we do not wish to preclude anyone from obtaining a copy.

Print vs Digital

When the Digital Revolution really got underway in the mid to late 1990s, the printing industry publications, the general magazines and general press were full of news of how digital would supplant print. (In fact, I only just came across a current article stating the same thing.) Ultimately "putting ink (or toner) on paper" would, with absolute certainty, be a thing of the past.

Having recently invested heavily in new printing presses, not to mention the digital book printing line we were about to install, we were quaking in our boots. Had we just committed the biggest blunder of our collective careers? Would we shortly be facing bankruptcy? These were just some of the questions we asked.

At about the same time, as a digression from our core business, we launched an eco-store, where we sold all manner of ecological and green products. It included an extensive book section. The predicament was that printed books were considered anything but "green". They were made from trees and the printing process was not deemed ecologically sensitive. Printed books were viewed as a thing of the past.

I wrote the introduction to the book section of the catalogue and website. In it I mused about this apparent contradiction. We were an eco-store and yet we were stocking and selling printed books. I pictured myself lying on a sofa in front of the fire with a laptop in the crook of my arm – instead of a printed book. I posited that I would much rather be leafing through the pages an actual book.

The Kindle and Tablet PCs came out. They had been stuff of science fiction. Once again, we feared for our future. Time went by and still we were printing books.

When it came to pass that we started writing books ourselves, we made the conscious decision to stick with print. We preferred printed books and so, we surmised, must others. However, not wishing to lose any potential reader, we also published them in Kindle format, as well as other eBook formats.

Research done over the past several years by the acclaimed PEW Research Centre has indeed come out proving what we have thought all along: ***Print books continue to be more popular than eBooks or audio books.*** To this day, about ¾ of people prefer printed books and digital appears to have flattened out.

Print books continue to be more popular than e-books or audio books

% of US adults who say they have ______ in the previous 12 months

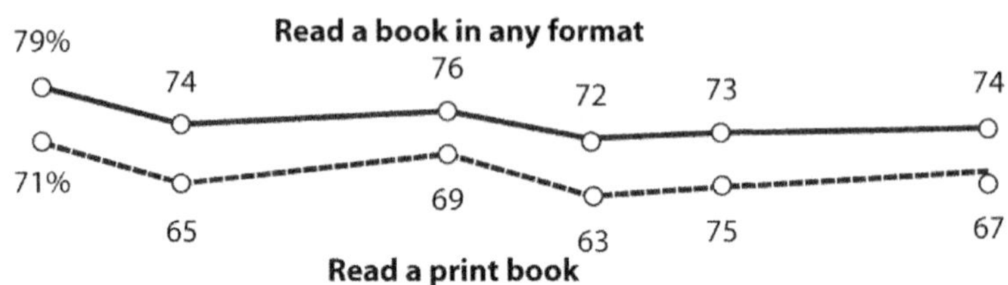

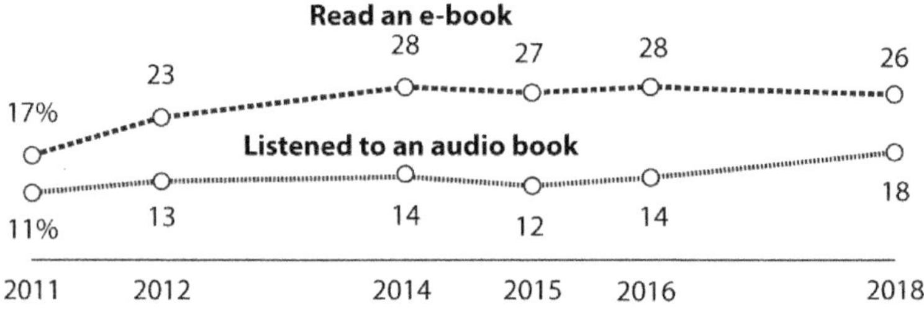

Source: Survey conducted January 3-10, 2018
PEW RESEARCH CENTER

The *PEW Book Reading 2018 Survey* goes on to point out some additional interesting information:

74% of Americans read books
Of those:
53% read only printed books
39% read both print and digital
and
9% read only eBooks

92% of book readers read printed books
49% of book readers read eBooks

eBook Formats

There are a lot of eBook formats, details of which can be found at:

http://en.wikipedia.org/wiki/Comparison_of_eBook_formats

For the purposes of self-publishing, the most commonly used are arguably: PDF, EPUB, Kindle and iBook.[28]

PDF

Adobe's Portable Document Format (PDF) with the filename extension .pdf was first introduced in 1993. It's a platform-independent means of exchanging fixed-layout documents. It quickly found wide adoption and using the free Adobe Acrobat reader, PDF files can be viewed on most devices.

Important attributes of PDF are that it maintains all layout and formatting. The user is able to fix the output image resolution and whether or not the entire font information of the used typefaces is included in the instruction set. The user is also able to determine if the document is editable or not. PDF is used in many print related workflows, such as those of KDP. It is an important element in self-publishing.

However, the fixed formatting also has negative implications for publishing as an eBook, as different devices have differing screen sizes. One must, therefore, scroll to see the whole page.

---

[28] See also: eBook Resources in the Appendix, as well as our chapter on eBook creation.

The newest versions of PDF include a "Tagged PDF." However, document reflow to fit different screen dimensions based on Tagged PDF, as opposed to re-flow based on the actual sequence of objects in the content-stream (as per the following file formats), is not yet commonly supported on mobile devices.

Re-flowable eBooks

All other eBook file types allow fully re-flowable text and other elements to accommodate different screen configurations and sizes. As mentioned earlier, how letters and symbols are displayed is coded into the file using what is called a mark-up language, much like a web page.

EPUB

EPUB is a technical standard for eBooks created by the International Digital Publishing Forum (IDPF). It is a vendor-independent XML[29]-based eBook format.

.epub files can be read by the Kobo eReader, BlackBerry devices, Apple's iBooks app running on Macintosh computers and iOS devices, Google Books app running on Android and iOS devices, Barnes & Noble Nook, Amazon Kindle Fire, Sony Reader and numerous other reading apps.

---

[29] Extensible Mark-up Language (XML) is a mark-up language that defines a set of rules for encoding documents in a format that is both human-readable and machine-readable. This means that things like type styles and the relative positioning of elements such as text or images to one another is defined in the underlying language.

Kindle

The Kindle eBook format is based on the Open eBook standard using XHTML.[30] The file extensions are .mobi[31] and .prc.

More on creating a file for Kindle in the following chapter *"eBook Creation"*.

iBook

The iBook format is a proprietary format from Apple Inc. It is based on, but different from, the EPUB standard. As it is proprietary, iBook eBooks created with Apple's free iBooks Author may only be sold through Apple.

eBook Creation

In the following we will describe in a few simple steps how to convert your book into an eBook. We will be describing the workflow for Microsoft Word®, which is the most common writing application and Adobe InDesign®, which is a sophisticated page and book design and layout application. As a finished file format, we will look at Kindle as the most common. We will then

---

[30] Extensible Hypertext Markup Language (XHTML) is part of the family of XML markup languages. It mirrors or extends versions of the widely used Hypertext Markup Language (HTML), the language in which Web pages are formulated.

[31] We have had issues uploading .mobi files to Joomla® powered websites. The workaround here is to rename the file to .prc, which is also accepted by Kindle devices.

also look at publishing your book via Smashwords[32] to access non-Amazon sales channels.

The best first step is to save the document out with a different name. This is to avoid overwriting the print book document.

As eBook readers vary greatly in size and configuration, the text and graphic elements must be able to reflow to fit the screen. The text pages of a book must therefore be reworked to allow this to happen.

Page layout:

First and foremost, the book needs to be reflowed into an A4 or letter sized document. This is the easiest way to see if the elements are formatted as per the following guidelines.

Table of Contents

Even if your printed book does not have one, your eBook should. The TOC generated in Word or InDesign keys in on the chapter headings. When the file is later exported to eBook format (see below) these TOC entries become hyperlinks a reader may use to find a particular place in your book.

---

[32] See chapter titled "*Selling your book on Smashwords*", which enables you to sell through major eBook retailers including Apple iBooks, Barnes & Noble, Kobo, Oyster, Scribd and others.

Text

As mentioned earlier, only the basic type styles will translate into the eBook: Normal, Caption and Headings. The only attributes you may assign to the running text are: Bold and Italic. If you resize text, this will be ignored.

Some tabs and indents will not work. Set up any indents in the styles.

Picture fonts (wingdings, dingbats, etc.) will not work. If these are needed, convert to images and place as images. This is explained in the section: *"Adding art elements to your document"*.

Images

Images and their comments should be "in line" with text and centred in the document. Images should not be left or right justified – text should not wrap around the images.

Placed image size is a potential issue. Experimentation may be necessary. For Kindle they seem to need to be larger, for other devices they may need to be smaller.

Colour images are allowed – even if your book is ostensibly black and white. As one might expect, the more modern eBook readers are fully colour capable.

Tables

Tables usually will not work in Kindle or other eBook formats. You have two options. You can rework the tables as bulleted points. Or, if the table formatting is essential, you can paste the table into Excel, rework the layout, and then convert this to an image file. You will find instructions for this under the heading: *Creating an art file from a Word or Excel document.*

Software Specific Considerations for eBook Creation

Adobe InDesign®

Once the above general steps have been completed, save the document with a different name to the actual book. Something like *Mybooktitle-eBook.indd* would work just fine. There are two easy workflows coming from InDesign[33].

Kindle Plugin (recommended)

System requirements:

- Windows XP, Vista, 7 or 10
- Intel Mac OSX 10.5 or later
- Adobe InDesign® versions CS4, CS5, CS5.5 or CS6[34]

---

[33] Guidelines for Kindle friendly InDesign file creation can also be found here: http://kindlegen.s3.amazonaws.com/KindlePluginForAdobeInDesign_HelpAndReleaseNotes.pdf

[34] Ed. note: I have found notes in forums re issues with CS4, but these were user issues that were resolved in each case.

For Mac users running OS X 10.6.7 or later, install the VeriSign Class 3 Code Signing 2010 CA to the "System" Keychain before installing the plugin[35].

Download the Plugin Here:

http://www.amazon.com/gp/feature.html?ie=UTF8&docId=1000765271

Installation is simple: Exit from InDesign and then run the installer.

Workflow

1. Open the InDesign document
   Note: The linked-in images are not required
2. Review for layered art – Images with type overlays, images with art overlays.
   a. Combine and flatten these images: Open the original images and combine using Photoshop®, save as .jpeg and replace in the document.
3. Export to Kindle
   File menu -> Export to Kindle
   a. With a big file such as a book with many photos, this may take about 5 minutes
   b. Don't worry about image resolution.
   c. Have a quick cup of tea.

The result of using the InDesign plugin is a .mobi file, which can be loaded right into a Kindle device, or uploaded to KDP (see below). Before uploading, it is

---

[35] Download the certificate from the Kindle Publishing Programs webpage at: https://kindlegen.s3.amazonaws.com/ VeriSignCA.cer
You will find instructions here:
http://kindlegen.s3.amazonaws.com/InstallingVeriSignCA.pdf

advised to preview and proof the book with a Kindle Previewer (see below).

ePub export

InDesign has a built-in .epub export facility. The workflow is the same as above.

KDP supports the uploading of unzipped .epub files. Before uploading, it is advised to preview and proof the book with a Kindle Previewer (see below).

To upload to **Smashwords** for most other eBook formats, export your manuscript to the .epub format. You can then upload this if it has been formatted to the Style Guide.

Microsoft Word®

Once the above general steps have been completed, save the document with a different name to the actual book. Something like *Mybooktitle-eBook.docx* would work just fine.

After that KDP will accept several different file formats: .kpf, .doc, .docx, .rtf and .html

Kindle Create .kpf files

Kindle Create is recommended by KDP. It will convert a MS Word document into a "reflowable" or *Print Replica Kindle Package Format* (.kpf) file.

You can download Kindle Create here:

https://kdp.amazon.com/en_US/help/topic/GHU4YEWXQGNLU94T

Word .doc, .docx and .rtf files

The simplest workflow is to upload your MS Word document file directly to KDP. This can work fine with documents that do not have complex formatting – which was theoretically removed in the preceding chapter *"eBook Creation"*.

HTML – Filtered Web Page

Perhaps the most versatile workflow is to save the file as "Web Page Filtered (*.htm, *.html)". This removes some of the Microsoft specific tags, which are wholly unnecessary.

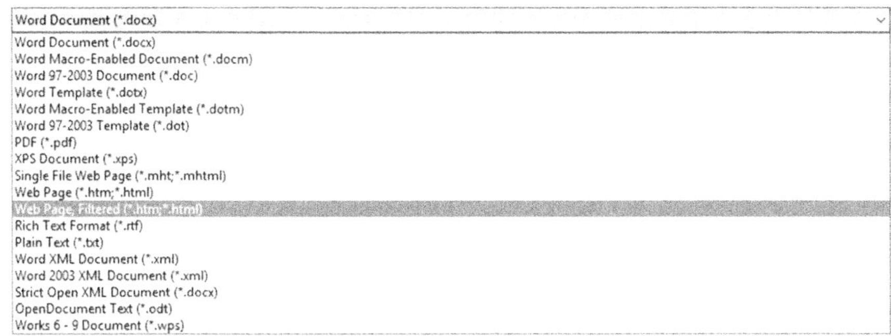

File conversion

In order to view the book on a Kindle device, the html file needs to be converted to a .mobi format. We would recommend using **Calibre** for this.

Calibre not only converts html files and eBooks into most formats, but it is also a library management tool for your eBooks – you can use it as your eBook reading platform. It is extremely easy to use.

It is a free (donations are appreciated) and open source eBook library management application developed by users of eBooks for users of eBooks. It has a cornucopia of features divided into the following main categories:

- eBook conversion
    - to most formats, including .mobi
- Library Management
- Synchronizing to eBook reader devices
- Downloading news from the web and converting it into eBook form
- Comprehensive eBook viewer
- Content server for online access to your book collection
- eBook editor for the major eBook formats

File previewing

Whereas the creation of an eBook file is easy, there can be a good deal of trial and error in getting the resulting file to look good. Some Microsoft Word® formatting does not work. The same also applies to Adobe InDesign®.

It is important to preview the resulting eBook file. There will inevitably be some problems with how it displays on the device. No matter how insignificant these problems seem, they do detract from the reading pleasure. These need to be corrected in the original application file, then saved out and converted to .mobi.

Amazon provides a free previewer that emulates all the current Kindle devices. Amazon Kindle Previewer is available here:

https://www.amazon.com/gp/feature.html?docId=1000765261

Amazon also provides a free Kindle Reading App that is available for virtually any non-Kindle device, including smart phones.

https://www.amazon.com/kindle-dbs/fd/kcp

Selling your eBook Online Using KDP

KDP is an eBook (and paperback book) self-publishing service that helps you publish your book the way you envision it. See: kdp.amazon.com

KDP allows you to publish your book your way, at zero cost, with no pressure to buy services you don't want or that don't help your process. There are many help files available that will walk you through the process, if for some reason you still have questions after reading this book. You will find many of these on our web page: https://www.whiteseahorse.ie/books

If you have not done so already, you will first have to have set up your account with KDP. This is described in detail in the chapter "Setting up your KDP account".

Getting started

If you have previously published your printed book on KDP and have created your .mobi file as per the preceding instructions, getting your Kindle eBook up on KDP is very easy. You start this process on your **Bookshelf** page.

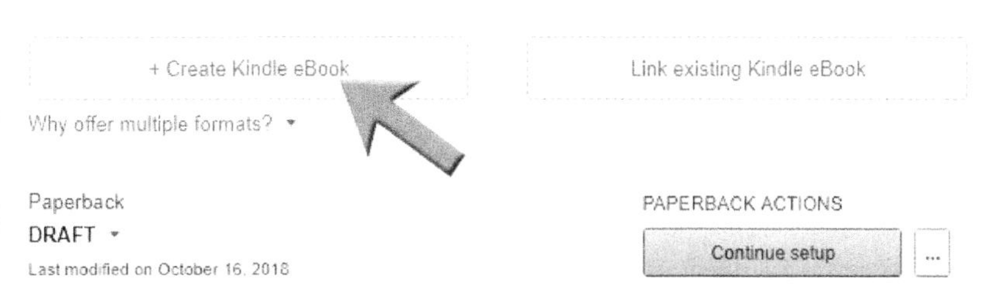

On your Bookshelf page click on "Create Kindle eBook" *next to your book.*

This will bring you to the **Kindle eBook Details** page, which will already have been pre-filled out based on what you entered for the print edition of the book.

If you have not yet, or do not wish to create and publish a print book, then you need to start near the top of your Bookshelf page.

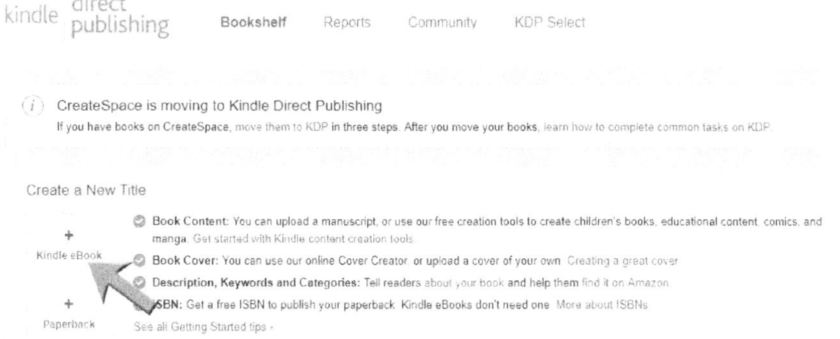

To start an eBook, click on the "Kindle eBook" *link near the top of your Bookshelf page.*

As above, this will bring you to the **Kindle eBook Details** page.

Kindle eBook Details Page

Here will select or enter all the information about your book.

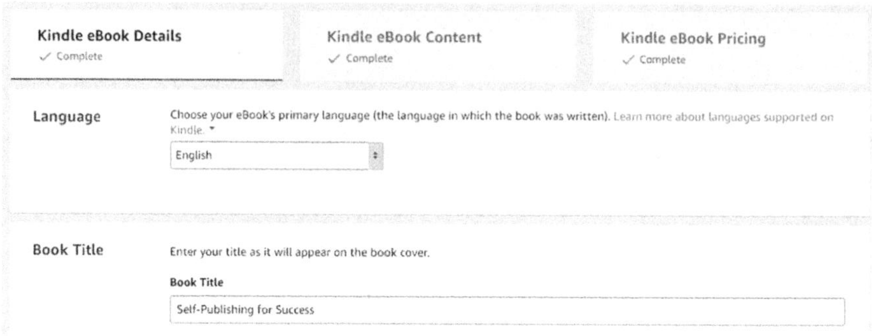

Notes:

- You may click on "Save as Draft" at any point in the process to save your work and do something else.
- Next to many items you will find a link. Clicking on this will provide some helpful information on what the item is intended for.
- The following information may already be filled in if you previously did so for the print edition of your book.

Language

From the drop-down menu select the language the book is written in. The default is English.

Book Title

Enter the book's title and sub-title if appropriate. As mentioned earlier, the title is very important. Research this thoroughly before continuing. If there are other similar titles, or if your book needs more description to differentiate it from other titles, then select a sub-title as well.

Series

Is the book part of a series? If so, is it the first? For example, we have set up "White Seahorse Classics" as an imprint. We use the Series Title to group them together on Amazon, as this appears as part of the title. In this case, we do not use a volume number.

Edition Number

If this is a title you have previously published, and this is an updated or revised edition, you may indicate this here also. A numeric entry is called for here. For example, this is the second edition of this book.

Author

Here you enter the name of the primary author. This can be an actual name or a pen name. It is under this name that the book will be sorted on Amazon.

Contributors

You may also add any number of co-authors, editors, illustrators and other optional contributors.

Description

"Description" is an important element where a good bit of wordsmithing is called for. This is a **description** of your title (max 4,000 characters, including spaces.) This is what people will see on Amazon. It is what they will base their purchasing decision on.

If space allows, you might add an **author biography**. This is your opportunity to introduce yourself and to state what makes you interesting, or your book worth reading.

Publishing Rights

Is this your own work, or are you reproducing a book from the public domain (out of copyright)? Our own Classics imprint falls under the public domain category.

Keywords

The **keywords** are essential to help people find your book. You may enter up to five keywords separated by a comma and a space. Your book title and your author name are separate from this, so do not repeat them. Try to avoid using terms such as: novel, or thriller. Instead use terms that actually key into the content of what you have written. These keywords will be added to your book's Amazon listing page as embedded meta tags. These are important and are how someone may find your book when searching on Amazon. The keywords are also catalogued by search engines like Google. This is how potential readers may find your book.

Categories

Think of Categories as sections in a book shop.

The Categories listed here are the Book Industry Standards and Communications (**BISAC**) categories are used by the book-selling industry to help identify and group books by their subject matter. Browse through the options and select two that work best for your book. If possible, try to avoid the catchalls such as "fiction/thriller". Wherever you can, it is best to stand out. Alternatively, if you know it, you may also enter the appropriate BISAC code.

Age and Grade Range

This is optional. If your book is targeted at a specific children's age range or if your book contains language, situations, or images inappropriate for children under 18 years of age, then you should select the appropriate minimums and maximums. For the US market this is a grade range.

Pre-order

This is only relevant if you wish to put your eBook 'out there' before you are entirely ready with it.

Once you have completed this simple form, you can click "Save as Draft", if you wish to do something else. Alternatively, you can click on "Save & Continue".

Kindle eBook Content Page

The Kindle eBook Content page has further selections for you to make.

Manuscript

An important first question here is whether you wish to apply **Digital Rights Management** (DRM) to your book. DRM is intended to inhibit unauthorized distribution of the Kindle file of your book. It protects your work from theft.

Some authors want to encourage readers to share their work and choose not to have DRM applied to their book. If you choose DRM, customers will still be able to lend the book to another user for a short period and can also purchase the book as a gift for another user from the Kindle store.

Note: Once you publish your book, you cannot change its DRM setting.

Manuscript upload

Having set up your manuscript in accordance with the guidelines described earlier, this is where you will upload your manuscript file. As explained, the recommended formats for Kindle eBooks are: .doc, .docx, .html, .mobi, .epub, .rtf, plain text, and .kpf. We have described our preferred workflow using .html and converting this to .mobi in the eBook Creation chapter.

Kindle eBook Cover

If you have already uploaded and processed your paperback book cover, it should appear here. If not, you have two options:

- Upload a cover file you have previously created. All you want here is the front cover, without the bleed, which you can crop out in photoshop. KDP accepts only .jpg or .tiff format files here.
- Launch the KDP Cover Creator and design your cover online as described in the chapter KDP Cover Creator. Bear in mind that it is just the front cover you are designing here.

Kindle eBook Preview

Once you have completed all of the preceding steps, you can (and should) preview your finished file. Even though you may already have done this as recommended above, this is very advisable to do it again, as KDP has processed the files you have uploaded.

Kindle eBook ISBN

An ISBN is not required for Kindle eBooks. Amazon will assign an ASIN (Amazon Standard Identification Number) to your Kindle eBook. This is a 10-character alphanumeric unique identifier assigned by Amazon.com and its partners for product identification within the Amazon organization.

However, if you have one for your book and wish to use it, you may optionally enter this number here. You may also enter the optional publisher information here.

For more information on ISBN, please see the appendix.

Kindle eBook Pricing Page

This page is where you determine how a reader may access your title and what you receive royalties for. As stated earlier, we believe it to our advantage to avail of as many sales channels (options) as possible to make our books available to potential customers.

KDP Select Enrolment

Enrolling your eBook in the optional KDP Select program gives you the opportunity to reach more readers and earn more money. If you enrol your book in **KDP Select**, it is automatically included in the Kindle Owners' Lending Library (KOLL) and Kindle Unlimited.

However, **any eBook enrolled in KDP Select may only be sold through the Kindle Store**. Yes, Amazon has introduced exclusivity. If the digital version of your book appears to be available for pre-order, for sale, or for free elsewhere (such as on your website or blog, or a third party's website), it is not eligible for KDP Select. You may continue to distribute/sell your book in any format other than digital; including print.

Enrolling in KDP Select gives you access to a set of promotional tools. You can schedule a Kindle Countdown Deal (limited time promotional discounting for your book) for books available on Amazon.com and Amazon.co.uk or a Free Book Promotion (readers worldwide can get your book free for a limited time).

The Kindle Owners' Lending Library (KOLL) allows people who have paid-for an Amazon Prime membership to read books for free. They may keep the title on their device for as long as they wish, or until the title has been withdrawn from KDP Select. Every time a unique customer reads pages in your book for the first time, you will be eligible for royalties. So, you are not giving your book away for nothing.

Kindle Unlimited (KU) is a subscription service available to Amazon customers. With Kindle Unlimited, customers can read as many books as they like and keep them as long as they want for a monthly subscription fee. They don't need to be Amazon Prime members. You will receive a share of the KDP Select Global Fund as individual customers read pages in your book for the first time.

Territories

Next, select which **territories** you have the distribution rights for or choose to sell your book in. As a self-published author, you in all likelihood own the worldwide rights. So, unless you have a particular reason to restrict the distribution, you should select "All territories."

Royalty and Pricing

Where things get a little confusing is under the **Royalty and Pricing** heading. Here you may enter the list price for your title and also select between 35% and 70% royalty plan. These do have differing implications which we will endeavour to explain.

KDP does provide a **pricing support**, which is based on past sales of similar books to the one you are publishing. Here is an example:

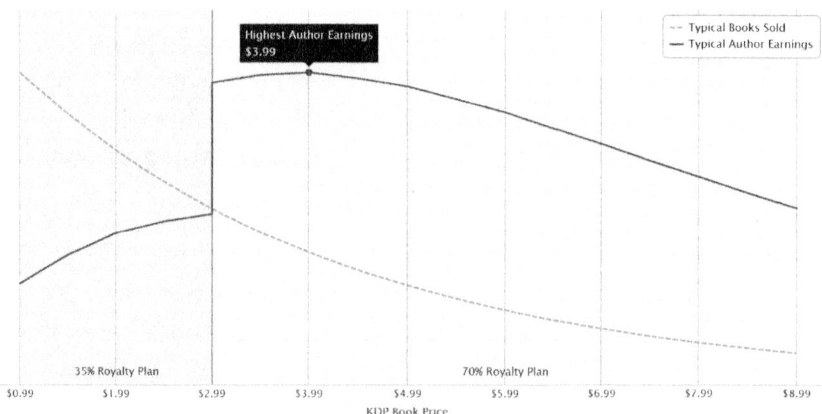

KDP is recommending $3.99 for this book

The base premise is that the lower the price of the eBook, the greater the sales volume will be – and conversely the higher the price the less you will sell.

If you then factor in that the 70% royalty band is restricted to sales between $2.99 and $9.99, there is a price point at which the royalties are theoretically the greatest. Note that the 70% bracket is not available in all territories. This bracket also does not include the delivery cost, which is based on file size.

For our own part, we looked at our printed book price, deducted the production (printing) cost and the estimated shipping cost and came to an eBook price of our own, which was indeed close to the KDP recommended price. We then opted for the 70% royalty bracket, as our pricing is always in this allowed price range.

Kindle MatchBook

The optional **Kindle MatchBook** gives customers who buy a print book from Amazon.com the opportunity to purchase the Kindle version of the same title for $2.99

or less. If you have a print version of your title on Amazon.com (through KDP), you can enrol the Kindle version in Kindle MatchBook and earn Kindle Direct Publishing (KDP) royalties based on the Promotional List Price (choose from $2.99, $1.99, $0.99, or free) for any Kindle MatchBook sale.

We have selected this for our books based on the understanding that we had already earned the maximum royalty when the printed book was sold. The reader would be unlikely to purchase the Kindle at face value but might be grateful if offered a special deal having bought the actual book. That way, we receive a little more cash, and everyone is happy.

Book Lending

The **Kindle Book Lending** feature allows users to lend digital books they have purchased through the Kindle Store to their friends and family. Each book may be lent once for a duration of 14 days and will not be readable by the lender during the loan period. Lending is only available for Kindle books purchased on Amazon.com.

All KDP titles are enrolled in lending by default. For titles in the 35% royalty option, you may choose to opt out of lending by deselecting the checkbox under "Book Lending" in the book pricing & promotion section of the title setup process, but you may not choose to opt out a 70% royalty optioned title.

Once you have completed all these steps and have agreed to the Ts & Cs, your book is ready to be published in Kindle format.

Selling Your Book Online Using Smashwords®

Smashwords provides global eBook distribution to major retailers and thousands of public libraries. It was created by author Mark Coker to make it fast, free and easy for any writer, anywhere in the world, to publish an eBook. It is reputedly the world's largest and the original, eBook distributor for indie authors.

> **Note** that if you have enrolled in the Kindle Select programme you may not sell your eBook here or through other outlets.

Smashwords is a fully automated system and automatically converts your title to all the major file formats. The one thing they interestingly do not provide is Digital Rights Management.

Once your book is accepted into the Smashwords Premium Catalogue, it is eligible for distribution to major eBook retailers including Apple iBooks, Barnes & Noble, Kobo, Oyster, Scribd and others. It will also be available for distribution to public libraries via OverDrive and Baker & Taylor Axis 360. With Smashwords you earn 60% of list price from major eBook retailers and up to 80% list at the Smashwords Store.

Setting up your account is as easy as might be expected. Once you have created a user name and password, you can create an author profile. Further down the account management page you can set up your Payment Settings. For residents of the US, payment is made either via paper check or PayPal. For residents outside the US, payment is made via PayPal only. Make sure your

PayPal account is set up correctly and that you can receive payments.

Formatting your book

Before you are able to publish your book via Smashwords, you must first do some work in formatting it. This is in addition to what we discussed in the chapter on eBook creation.

Smashwords does accept EPUB files. However, this is only for sale in the .epub format. EPUB files are not converted to the other formats.

The only file format that is accepted for conversion to all file types is Microsoft Word .doc. If you are using a newer version of Word, then you must save your file as Word 97-2003.

The system is very particular about the document formatting. They do provide an excellent and very detailed free style and formatting guide which is well worth studying in depth before proceeding.

https://www.smashwords.com/books/view/52

Your best starting point is the Word document you worked on for your Kindle book. Do not try to use the .html file you created from this, as the images will not display.

Tables

Besides the considerations listed in the eBook creation chapter, it is important to note that Smashwords will not accept any tables whatsoever. KDP (Kindle) is more tolerant here. So, you will need to go through your book and remove and rework all tables, if you have not done so before. As mentioned in the Kindle chapter, you can either convert tables into images or use bulleted text. Conversion to images is discussed under the heading: *"Creating an art file from a Word or Excel document".*

Table of Contents

Whereas it is advised in the creation of a Kindle file to use the MS Word generated Table of Contents (TOC), Smashwords will not accept this. The TOC must be recreated from scratch. In a book with many headings (like this one) this can be a lot of work (ouch). In the long term this is a worthwhile exercise, as it is the difference between being able to publish in these additional channels or not.

In their formatting guide Smashwords advises to key in all the chapter heads where the TOC is supposed to go. Rather than keying in the entire Table of Contents, we have found it easier to copy the Word generated TOC and paste this into Notepad on the PC or TextEdit on the Mac. This strips out all the hyperlinks. You will need to delete all the page numbers from the table of contents as these are irrelevant in an eBook. When this is done, copy the text back into the book document where you wish the TOC to appear.

Then one is instructed to go to the actual chapter heads and insert bookmarks (Insert-Links-Bookmark).

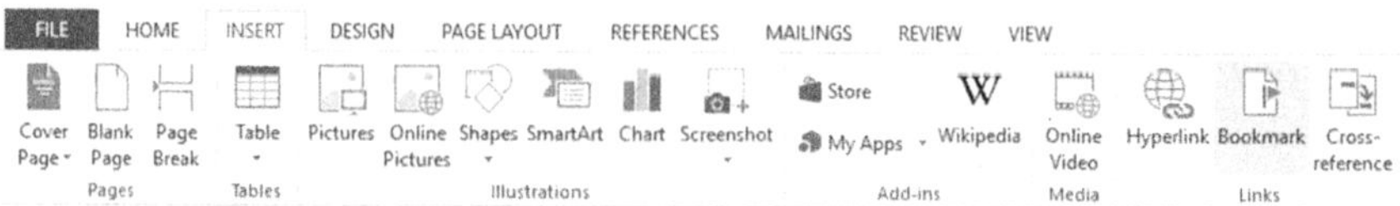

Each bookmark needs to be named. The name cannot have spaces, numbers, or any non-alpha characters other than an underscore "_".

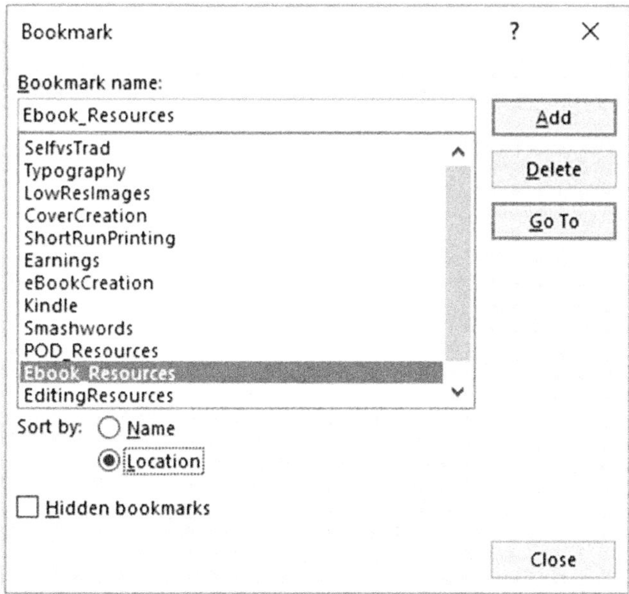

Link each TOC entry to the appropriate bookmark. To do this, select a TOC heading, right mouse click and then select Hyperlink – or click on Hyperlink in the above-mentioned Link area.

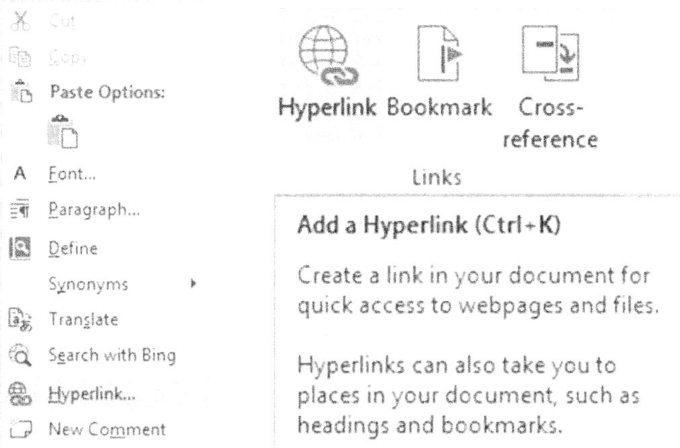

A new window will pop up. On the left side of this click on “Place in this Document”. A list of all the bookmarks previously defined will be available. Select the one you wish to link to and click OK.

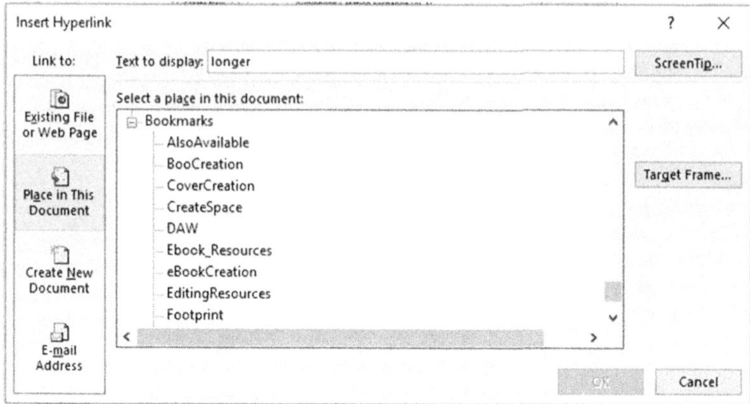

With a longer TOC, we found this to be quite cumbersome, as Word sorts the bookmarks alphabetically, unless you sort them by location.

Instead of creating all these new bookmarks, we found it acceptable to highlight the text heading in the new TOC and add a hyperlink as in the preceding.

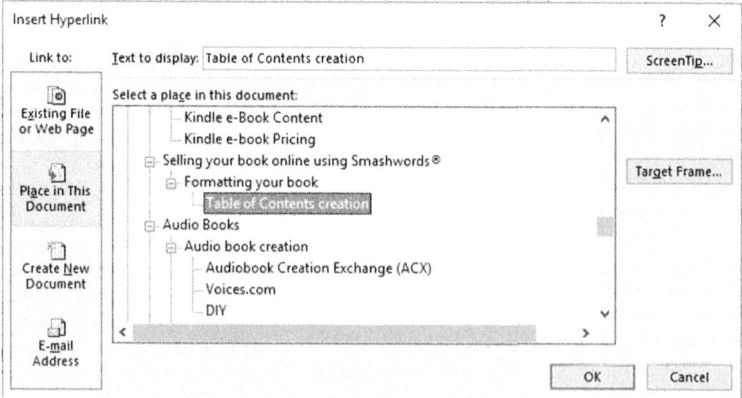

The only difference is that you scroll down through the listed headings and link the TOC heading with the actual heading.

Once the table of contents has been recreated, the document can be saved out and uploaded – remember to save as Word 97-2003 .doc file format.

Images

One other thing is that Smashwords restricts the file size of the .doc format document to a maximum of 15MB. If your book has images in it, you will quickly exceed this. You are, therefore, advised to reduce the size of all the images as described earlier in the chapter on creating your book.

Publishing on Smashwords

Before starting to fill out the "Publish your Book" form, it is advised to read through it to have an idea of what you need to have "at the ready." There is no option to save your work in progress while you find some information or adjust a file you wish to upload.

By all means click on the provided links to further information and to review their terms and conditions at this time as well. If you do this while filling out the form and preparing to upload your files you may lose information you have previously entered.

We found it very useful to open (and save out) a text file in Notepad (PC) or TextEdit (Mac) in advance. We use this to collect all the information we want to enter into the form:

- Book Title
- Long Description
- Short Description

- Price
- Keywords

We do this so that we don't have to go out and find or rewrite this again bit by bit from scratch.

Pricing

Having already put some consideration into the pricing of our Kindle eBook, we think it prudent to charge the same amount for our books on Smashwords.

Of interest is that you may make a portion of your book available as a free sample. This 'try before you buy' scheme provides an incentive for a reader to get a good idea of how your book reads prior to buying it.

Royalties are 85% of net proceeds by Smashwords

Non-affiliate sales: Sales direct to customers via Smashwords. Royalties are 85% of list price less the PayPal processing fee.

Affiliate sales: Sales by individuals who choose to promote your books and make money. Royalties are 70.5%. Authors may opt out of sales through affiliates.

Premium Catalogue Retailers: Sales through Apple (operates Apple Book Stores in 51 countries), Barnes & Noble (US and UK), Scribd, Kobo, Blio, and others. Royalties are around 42% depending on the reseller.

Audio Books

Perhaps the most important reason to consider doing an audio book is that it lends immense credibility to your title. The perception is that only the big publishers can do one. It makes you look "professional."

As a "reader", audio books are a great way to immerse yourself in a novel or other title while actively doing something else – like driving a car, sitting on a train on the way to work, working out, cooking, or convalescing from an illness. Some people do not like reading but enjoy listening. There are others with dyslexia and those who are blind and cannot read.

The fact is, that people do spend a good deal of money on audio books; according to the Audio Publishers Association, the 2017 sales came to an estimated $2.5 billion, up 21.5% over 2016! Latest estimates indicate that there was a further rise of 22.7% in 2018. The audio book is thus a potentially very viable additional sales channel.

As with the relationship between eBooks and printed books, there is a similar relationship with audio books. People who purchase one are potential customers for another version.

Audio book creation

A few years ago, producing any audiobook was expensive and time consuming. Publishers would only produce audio books for their best-selling titles. Today there are services that make producing an audiobook relatively cheap and easy. An audio book can be a simple recording or professionally done by voice-over artists.

Audiobook Creation Exchange (ACX)

ACX (ACX.com) is the leader in self-published audiobooks. It is a service for publishers, authors, agents and rights holders to connect with professional narrators and create audiobooks. ACX is owned and operated by Audible Inc., an Amazon company. All titles produced through ACX are made available for sale on Audible.com, Amazon.com and iTunes.

ACX has a "DIY workflow", which allows users who own the rights to already completed audiobooks to upload them to ACX and have them distributed through Audible's sales channels. They do have guidelines on the creation of the audio book that must be adhered to.

ACX offers a very wide spectrum of publishing deals. They even let you produce the audiobook for free, provided you split the revenue with the narrator 50/50.

Voices.com

Voices.com is a resource of over 200,000 voice recording artists, covering a wide range of voice-over work, including audio books. It is a resource for finding a voice talent that fits your work and paying for their services in a secure online environment.

You can post a job and receive responses based upon the specific project requirements. The system analyses your needs with matching voice talent profiles and invites only the most qualified candidates to respond to a job posting. Their search engine helps you to search for voice talent by keyword, gender, experience and location.

DIY Audiobooks

If you prefer to do your own voice recording, bear in mind that this involves a lot of hard work. Having said that, authors of how-to, self-help and other non-fiction titles may wish to consider this, as it increases their stature as the expert in their particular field. (See also the chapter on Platform.)

There are a number of fully featured commercial computer programmes called Digital Audio Workstations (DAW) available to do your own recording. Please see the appendix for a list of available commercial programmes.

There are also some free and open-source DAW programmes. Here are two examples:

- **Audacity** is a digital audio editor that can run on most operating systems. In addition to recording audio from multiple sources, Audacity can be used for post-processing of all types of audio, including podcasts by adding effects such as normalization, trimming and fading in and out. www.audacityteam.org
- **Rosegarden** is a multi-featured audio application only for Linux[36] that includes audio mixing plugins, a notation editor and MIDI.[37] www.rosegardenmusic.com

Just remember that the quality of your microphone as well as a sound-proofed environment will make a huge difference in the quality of your recording.

---

[36] Linux is a Unix-like computer operating system assembled under the model of free and open-source software development and distribution.

[37] MIDI (Musical Instrument Digital Interface) is a technical standard that describes a protocol, digital interface and connectors and allows a wide variety of electronic musical instruments, computers and other related devices to connect and communicate with one another.

Selling your audio book

Setting up your own catalogue for secure sales and downloading the audio file is a lot of work; we tried that. Unless you have a large volume of titles, building your own catalogue is not worth the effort. There are secure, easy to use sales platforms for audio books, that in some instances you may tailor to your needs. The three major audiobook sales channels are: Audible, Amazon and iTunes.

Audible

Audible (an Amazon company) is the world's largest producer of downloadable audiobooks. Audible sets the price for the audio books. Audible may discount audio books substantially and offer low subscription pricing. Royalties are based on actual sales pricing.

Audible's .aa file format includes unauthorized-playback prevention by means of an Audible user name and password. The downloaded book can be used on up to four computers and three smartphones at a time. Licenses are available for schools and libraries.

iTunes

iTunes is, of course, huge in the audio marketplace. Setting up a publisher account is, however, cumbersome. There are several requirements that must be met before Apple will approve an account. It may therefore be advisable to work with an aggregator. These are Apple-approved experts in delivering content to iTunes. For a fee, they can correctly format and deliver your content to Apple's specifications. Apple has published a list of approved aggregators at:

https://itunespartner.apple.com/en/music/partnersearch

DIY Marketing

Marketing is not selling; marketing precedes sales. To paraphrase Harvard Business School's retired professor of marketing Theodore C. Levitt:

Marketing has less to do with getting potential readers to pay for your book than it does establishing that it exists and developing a desire to read it; thus, developing a demand for your book to fulfil the reader's needs.

As a self-published author, when it comes to getting your book to the reader, you must be your own marketer. In order to sell copies of your book, you must first get the word out about it. In this you are, at least initially, on your own. You need to make a commitment to invest real time in marketing. Marketing is hard: it's an entirely different kind of challenge to writing a book. More important, marketing a book starts long before the book releases. To reiterate: whereas sales may follow, they have little to do with marketing.

There are two often misinterpreted catchwords we need to review to create an understanding of the marketing process:

Platform
and
Footprint

Your Platform

If you have ever been to a publisher's website to research the possibility of submitting your work to them, you may have seen a question about your "platform." The reality is that this is something you have unwittingly been working on your entire life. **Your platform is all about you.** It is what you have done or created in the past that is connected with your current work, what you are currently doing that is relevant to this work and who you can reach that has a connection with or an interest in what you are doing.

The key thing to remember is that **your platform is subject specific**. Think of it as a column with you on top of it. The taller the column, the better you will be seen.

Your Platform helps you
stand out above the crowd

The term 'platform' is particularly relevant to non-fiction. If over time you have become the expert in a particular field, people will actively seek you out for advice. In turn they will gravitate towards your writing.

This can be equally true for writers of fiction. As an example, there are several authors that I follow. Their platform is in a particular genre. I take note if they have a speaking engagement or bring out a new book. If there is a radio interview, I try to catch it or listen to the podcast.

Your platform results from the body of your work in a specific field or genre. If you produce great work, this will significantly strengthen your platform. Building a platform is a long-term process. You need to say meaningful things about either yourself, your industry, or your subject matter. Just being loud can do your platform more harm than good. Be honest, speak from your heart, make sure you entertain and also educate.

We understand that writing (anything) comes from deep inside you. It makes you vulnerable. You are subjecting yourself to criticism. Yet to create and build your platform you must be seen to be heard. You must be visible.

Whether you are working online or using traditional media, there are several questions you need to ask yourself:

- Where do you or your work regularly appear?
- What communities are you a part of?
- Who do you influence?
- How many people see your message?
    - How does the word spread?
    - Where does it spread to?
- Are you reaching your target audience with the message about your work or your book?
    - Is your book relevant to the audience?
    - How are you reaching the audience?

If you write in more than one genre, you will have a separate platform for each. For example, mine are:

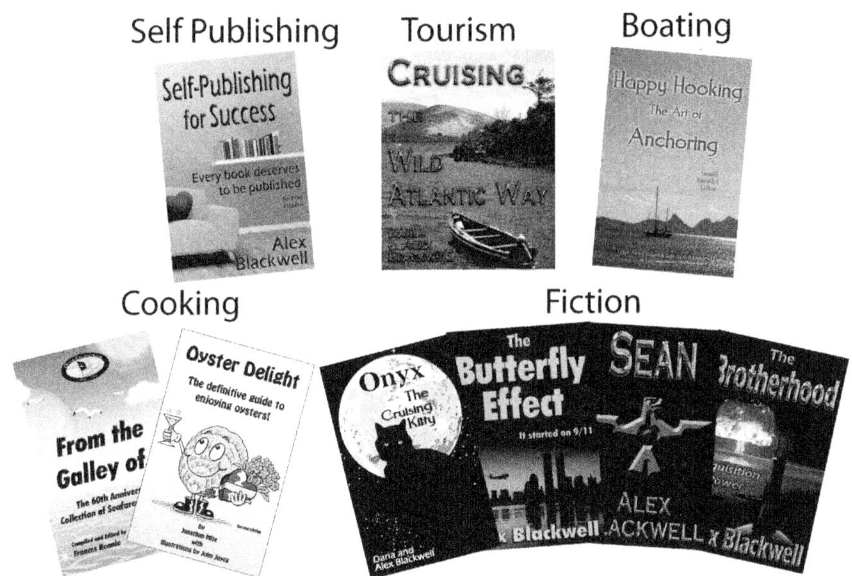

Your Footprint

Footprint is often confused with your platform. Your platform is always on-topic. As mentioned previously, you may have several platforms depending on the breadth of your work. However, your footprint includes all your platforms and extends beyond that. **Your footprint is who you are: everything you have done or created in the past and anything are currently doing**.

Your footprint is your brand – it is you. As an author, you are a public person. Anything you say or do is seen and noted. This literally and figuratively becomes part of your footprint.

You can view your platform as a silo, with your book's subject and your expertise as its base. Consider your footprint as a field with one or more silos in it. Around the silos are all the other things you do, write, or say. The bigger the field, the more extensive your footprint.

Everything you do or create may build interest in something else you have written. In a retail environment, this is called cross-merchandising. Look at the back of this book. There you will find a list of the other books we have written. They cover all sorts of different topics. A reader who likes a non-fiction title such as this one, may be interested in another topic we have written about. He or she may also wish to check out one of our novels – and visa-versa.

So, what is the best way to increase the sales of an individual title? Keep writing. Publish another book and another. Write articles, do blogs, get yourself out there. This is much like what was discussed under "Platform", but you are not bound to a subject.

We also went a step further. We launched a classics imprint. Here we are re-releasing out of copyright classic novels that we like to read. These push back to our publishing website expanding our reach for potential readers of our own books.

Your Footprint is you as an overall author and you as a person. If you have a website, you will include an author page – about you and all your diverse interests and writings.

Your Footprint should not have conflicting points of view. If it does, consider publishing under different pen names. A good example of this is Nora Roberts who writes romance novels. She writes murder mysteries under the pen name JD Robb. Similarly, JK Rowling is the author of the Harry Potter series of books. For adult novels she pens under the pseudonym Robert Galbraith.

Internet & Social Media

In today's world, the internet is your biggest asset when it comes to working on your platform. The internet is a huge equalizer. It is your opportunity to be on an even playing field with the biggest publisher.

So how do you get the internet and social media to work for you? Start with some basic market research.

Use Google to find relevant websites, chat rooms and forums. Search social media sites for relevant discussion groups. Compile a list of places that are relevant to your work and could potentially showcase your expertise. If you respond to relevant questions, join discussions and post meaningful articles or excerpts from which people can learn or be entertained, they will be inclined to search for more from you.

You do not want to just post ads for your work or about your book. This is considered spamming and will turn other people away.

Another option is to find partners searching for relevant content to post or publish on their platforms. If you can find outlets for published articles either online or in print, you will always be permitted to cite your published work in association with the article. Being associated with independent sources does wonders to build your platform and create demand for your book.

Following are some of the online platform building options you have. You do not have to do them all. The more bases you cover the greater your exposure.

Website

You have several options when it comes to building a website. As with your book, it deserves to be properly designed and laid out. A website today does not have to cost a great deal of money. With publishing solutions like WordPress and Blogger, you can create a fine-looking website; one that even functions adequately as a storefront, for free. There are standard templates and widgets built into the software that enable anyone with a small amount of technical expertise and a bit of persistence to create a professional-looking website.

If you need help, you should be able to hire a young web developer to work with you locally for less than $30 or €30/hour.

You not only need to develop and maintain the website, but above all keep updating it to keep it current. The more often your website is updated, the more likely it is to rise to the top of search results.

For non-fiction, the website can be subject related.[38] This is where you might publish related articles, excerpts from your book and information on your subject related activities.

You may also consider an author or publishing site.[39] This is where you publish your title listings, information about your books, as well as your author bio.

Include advertisements on each page for your books with links to your listings on Amazon and elsewhere. Make

---

[38] For our sailing and boating related writing we maintain a large website: www.Coastalboating,net – the boater's resource for places to go and things to know.

[39] Our publishing site is www.whiteseahorse.ie – Where dreams take flight and become reality.

sure each page has the appropriate metatags: Keywords and Description. All images should be sized correctly and have relevant 'Alt' tags. Ensure the content is relevant.

How do you get traffic to your website? By leveraging your platform. Blog on bigger sites that aggregate bloggers or podcasts. Post about your articles etc on social media. It takes time to build up traffic, but sincere voices will always rise to the top.

Your blog

How does a blog differ from a website? A blog (or weblog) is a regularly updated web page that is written in informal or conversational style. So, whereas your website has the formal description of your book and how to buy it, the blog may take the reader on a journey about how you developed your idea and wrote the book.

If possible, you should include or link your active blog into your website – aim at one good article a week. The more you put out there, the more traffic you will bring in and the more exposure your books will attain.

This can be the centre of your online universe. It is where you put out new ideas, run surveys and interact with commenters. Of course, every time you add a blog entry, tweet about it (as opposed to about your book) and put it up on Facebook.

You can offer more interaction after the reader opts in – and joins your **mailing list**. Your blog is also where you may keep a schedule of author events and promotional appearances.

Forums

In a way, a Forum is a group blog. People meet in one online space to discuss a particular subject. As an expert in your field, it is important to demonstrate this to others who may have a need or interest in your expertise. Monitor online forums where questions may come up that are relevant to your knowledge. Your "signature" may elude to this expertise. Your website and book can also be mentioned discreetly. The more you participate and help others, the more you will be respected and sought out when the need arises.

Facebook

Facebook is a friend-based social media platform that enables you to interact with individuals and groups. It is the largest social networking site with 2.27 billion members as the third quarter of 2018. As it is truly real-time interactive. It is very different from a web page or a blog. Facebook is a pull medium. It enables you to intercept 'friends' when they are online 'in the room with you' and bring them to your page or your message.

You can build your own page,[40] announce new events about your books and post photos and links to related subject matter. Similarly, you can comment on other people's postings on their page and join subject related discussions. The latter are vital as they help build your platform showing that you are indeed the expert.

---

[40] We have a page for each of our non-fiction titles. We also have pages linked to our two primary websites

If you are brave, start your own discussion group. This can generate many thousands of followers but requires constant monitoring and contributions. You may set up your Facebook store on shopify.com. You can share a particular post with groups who may be interested. They may then, in turn, come to your Facebook page or website to see more. You can also pay for advertisements that are displayed to a selected target audience.

Twitter

Twitter is frequently maligned but can be very powerful. It is a push medium as opposed to pull. It pushes your up to 280-character message out to the masses – anyone who may be listening. That is why it is so effective in creating political and social movements.

As an author, tweet about things that interest you. Tweet about articles by others relevant to your work as well as things you have written about. Include images. They make your tweet stand out better. They do not count as characters. On occasion, do also tweet about your own work and actual book – just don't do it constantly. That is considered spam and is seriously frowned upon. Finely crafted quotes from your work can be easily propagated if people like them enough to retweet to their followers. Always include a link to a relevant page on your website.

Twitter enables you to gather a following of people in your niche. More important, it enables you to target people, who may not be following you, but are interested in a particular subject, by using the invaluable hashtag. For example, anyone searching for information on #boating, #sailing, #writing or #selfpublishing will encounter your tweet if you tagged it. Once again, it is important to tweet routinely. In doing so, you drive traffic to your own website every day.

You can also interact with thought leaders. One of the most respected authors on Twitter is JK Rowling. She is a master of the art and it pays to follow her and study her style.

Readers Gazette

Readers Gazette is a website designed to give self-published authors better coverage in the book world using Twitter as their promotional tool. You may join Readers Gazette and add your (digital) books at no cost. @Readersgazette and @RGBookworld will then periodically send out tweets about your books.

LinkedIn

LinkedIn is a business oriented social media platform. On LinkedIn you can participate in discussions with professionals with specific affiliations or credentials and ask questions in groups of which you are a member. Subject related groups on LinkedIn are particularly valuable for non-fiction genres.

You may also run your own groups and build a large network of business professionals in your specialty. Gaining a reputation and following on LinkedIn is extremely valuable.

Instagram

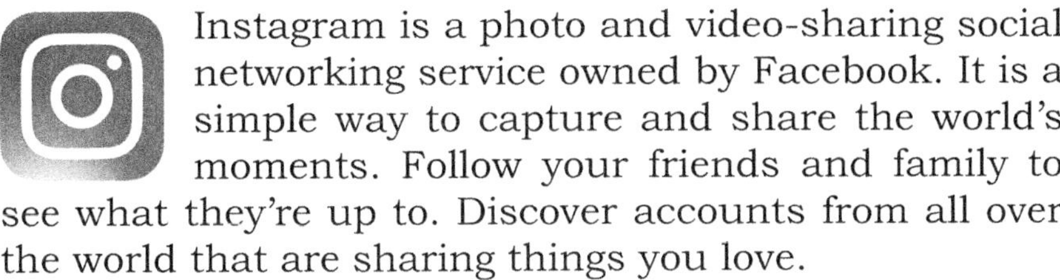

Instagram is a photo and video-sharing social networking service owned by Facebook. It is a simple way to capture and share the world's moments. Follow your friends and family to see what they're up to. Discover accounts from all over the world that are sharing things you love.

You can, of course also use Instagram to post photos and stories about your book or writing work.

Google Books

Google Books enables the contents of your book to be databased and come up in the result of a Google search. Whereas this only enables the searcher to read short parts of your book, it does expose them to it. A link is then provided to purchase your book.

YouTube

If you are up to creating in-topic videos, then using YouTube provides you with a huge resource to build a bigger platform and reach out to more people. YouTube is quickly gaining ground on Facebook and is the number two social networking site with 1 billion unique visitors (Feb 2017).

You can create a personal channel, post videos with tips, answers to common questions, walkthroughs and just about anything else you can think of. You can gather subscribers and stay in touch with regular updates.

Pinterest

Pinterest is a social media web and mobile application company that operates a software system designed to discover information on the World Wide Web, mainly using images and, on a smaller scale, GIFs and videos. Pinterest has reached 250 million monthly active users as of October 2018. Pinterest is also used to promote products and drive sales by posting appropriate images.

Goodreads (Shelfari)

Goodreads lets you interact with a book-loving community. You can find information on author events, share your own reading adventures with other readers and build a community of your own. Similar to Amazon, Goodreads is a common place for people to write a review about your title once they have read it. Here you can have an author page as well as a member (book reader) page.

Author Central

amazon AuthorCentral

Amazon's author page gives you the opportunity to post your resume and a photo. You can link in all your titles. If a reader likes your work, or is interested in you, your author page becomes your presence on Amazon.

Remember to claim your title. All of this increases your footprint. Remember also that each Amazon property requires its own author page.

Book trailer

Of course, if possible, you should also do a book trailer and post it on YouTube and your website or blog. This can be a visually stimulating clip about your book or a reading of the first chapter or a short section. A rule of thumb for a trailer is that it should only be about one minute in length. Any longer and people may lose interest. Be sure to include a detailed written description so the search engines pick it up.

Podcast

If well done, an audio podcast can be an excellent vehicle to introduce a subject or a story (novel). The podcast may be lengthier, as in the audio from a seminar, or a reading from your book. As with a video, there are widgets you can add to your web page enabling people to listen to your podcast.

Articles

In this exploding world of online resources, content is gold. Experts are in high demand. Your platform is all about maintaining the impression that you are the expert in your field. So, write articles for online magazines, which are called ezines. At the end of the articles you can add your 'signature,' which will include reference to your published work, your website or your Facebook page. You might even get paid for the articles you write, especially if they are published in print magazines associated with the ezines.

Many writers of fiction write articles about what they are expert in: the creative process, grammar and punctuation, overcoming writer's block and so on. Their fiction may also be based on an expertise. For example, Clive Cussler is an active adventurer, leading expeditions, finding shipwrecks, etc. – much like the heroes in his books. Similarly, short stories that get published can be exceptional promotion for other writing, such as your novel.

Webinars

A webinar is basically a live seminar, presentation, or lecture over the internet. This is an excellent way for you to deliver your expertise without leaving your office or home.

There are several applications that can enable you to do this by yourself. Depending on your field of expertise, there are also organizations that will connect presenters with potential viewers. For example, we do our boat anchoring webinar with several international boating organizations. They have each licensed the software and then bring in an audience from their membership. We make a little money after each webinar, but the main objective is to continue to build our platform and sell our books.

Email list

As you build your platform, you will have the opportunity of interacting with people from many places. Whenever you get a chance, offer the people you communicate with, or are presenting to, the opportunity of joining your mailing list. If people opt in, they will in all likelihood be pleased to receive news or updates from you. They are, after all, your target audience.

If you use a list (purchased or otherwise) of recipients who did not request your information, then do not be surprised if you receive negative or even threatening feedback.

Book reviews

One of the most important things you can do to increase your title's visibility is to have it reviewed. Just remember that you are "putting yourself out there." They may give you a bad review. It can also take a long time before they review your title – remember that someone actually has to read the book and they probably have a long list of titles ahead of yours in the queue.

There are reviewing blogs as well as paid-for services. Some of them are excellent.

However, always carefully read their policy before submitting. It is a lot of work reviewing a book. The partnership between a reviewer and an author is very personal. An author must enter this relationship with all due respect.

If someone has said they did not want to review your work, don't ask them again – even if you messed up your first request. If someone declines reviewing your work, or worse pans it, accept this and go away quietly. Raising a fuss will only create enemies and negative publicity. That is one thing no author can afford.

Take the time to write a personal letter if you are looking for a review. A one-to-many letter (boilerplate) that does not address the reviewer personally is insulting and can only result in a rejection.

If someone does review your work, let the world know. This shows your appreciation and also helps the reviewer. Share their review on Facebook and retweet their review on Twitter – don't just "Like" it. Send them a separate note and/or a tweet to say, "thank you." They spent a lot of time reading your book and thinking about it; good manners helps solidify a good relationship.

Email signature

Sending an email is not only a way of communicating, but also a way to deliver a subtle advertisement to the recipient, who may indeed be a potential customer.

As we have both fiction and non-fiction titles and the non-fiction in particular address different population segments, we have several different email signatures. One for each of our silos. We also have a general publishing one that lists all books. We select the one most appropriate for the recipient for each email we send.

"Traditional" Media

Don't forget more traditional forms of promoting your work. A review in the local paper or your local radio station can sometimes be the start of something bigger. We have been interviewed by our local papers and on the local radio. These have been about one or another of our books and have also been about our exploits. Each time, we have seen a spike in book sales.

The same applies to trade journals or subject-related magazines. We are frequent contributors to several sailing and boating magazines. Some we are paid-for and some we are not. In either case, we always include a by-line that mentions our relevant book titles.

Service Providers

Service providers are there to provide you with a service. Yes, they want your money, and some might indeed be classified as 'sharks'. But there are good ones and they can provide you value. As long as you remain aware of the costs and benefits: **Approach self-publishing as a business** and keep an open mind, even a shark may become your ally.

Bottom Line: ***Be aware of sharks****.*
(Image borrowed from Finding Nemo)

Vanity Press, Book Marketing, & Promotion Agencies

As a past short-run book printer, we dealt with several Vanity Publishers and Book Marketers. Their business is to take a title, edit it, design the contents and cover, produce the books and help market the title. For each of these steps the author pays a fee. Some Vanity presses may also distribute the books and actually pay a royalty if any are sold.

For many authors, this is a soul destroying and expensive way to go. The books are often churned out, printed and shipped to the author. As described earlier under "Short Run Printing", the author then then sits on stacks of cartons of books.

If the author opts for the trade show option, their book may actually be displayed at a show. There it will be placed on a shelf along with many other titles managed by the agency. The chances of anyone seeing it are usually slim.

Of course, besides paying for the space at the show, the author must also pay for copies of his or her book to be given away as review copies. As anyone who has ever been to a book show can attest, it is a great place to acquire countless free books. Some attendees actually walk around towing hand-trucks or suitcases to accommodate the books they are taking home.

A friend of ours went to a promotion agency with her first novel. They helped with editing, cover design, printing, radio interviews, a website, print interviews and even a book launch. We believe she has dropped around £8,000 to date.

Vanity Presses, Book Marketing and Promotion Agencies are very good at promoting their services. As such their offerings often include terms such a "value-added", "silver", "gold", or "platinum package." Almost all of the options offered in the packages are things that one might think would be included as a matter of course.

Points to consider

There may well be things you need assistance with. Most agencies also offer "a la carte" services in addition to their package deals. (There are also freelancers who can be of assistance.) It is worth considering a few points on the services agencies may or may not offer to avoid being eaten by a shark:

1. **ISBN**
   Although cumbersome, an author can obtain their own ISBN[41] from their local country agency at a nominal cost. Having your own ISBN number has only one advantage: it makes you the "Publisher of Record." If you self-publish with the likes of KDP or Smashwords, the ISBN is provided free of charge. You still retain the copyright. Agencies will charge for providing a number. If it is nominal, this can be acceptable as they are recouping costs.
2. **Copyright**
   If your country is a signatory to the Berne Convention[42] – and that covers most countries in the world – then your work is protected from the moment you create it in a format that is "perceptible either directly or with the aid of a machine or device."
   That means that you automatically own the copyright to any original work you create – as long as you commit it to readable form, which you have done as a self-published author. There is no charge for this.
3. **Library of Congress Control Number (LCCN – US only)**
   US authors may wish to register their title with the Library of Congress. It expedites book processing by US libraries and book dealers who

---

[41] See appendix for more information on ISBN

[42] The Berne Convention for the Protection of Literary and Artistic Works, usually known as the Berne Convention, is an international agreement governing copyright, which was first accepted in Berne, Switzerland, in 1886.

obtain copies of the book. There is some paperwork involved. The Library of Congress does charge a nominal amount. It also requires a copy of the book (pdf or print), that is non-returnable. If you engage someone to register your book for you, it is reasonable to pay for this service.

4. **Press Releases**

   A press release is something that is written in a specific format for the press to repurpose. If you engage someone to do this for you, it is reasonable to pay for this service. Just ensure that they write about your book and do not issue some generic, regurgitated text. You can also write and distribute your own press releases.

5. **Trailer**

   As stated earlier, a trailer for your book is a good thing to have. If you are fairly familiar with Microsoft PowerPoint®, or other software such as Animoto®, then this is something you can do yourself. You might also consider hiring a professional – a service you will pay for.

6. **Catalogue**

   This is not something you should pay for. Your Amazon listing is already a catalogue listing. Other free catalogues include Goodreads, etc. An agency's catalogue is in all likelihood not going to give you any value for money.

7. **Publicity and PR**

   This is, by all means, something you can do yourself. If you want help, do get a good and clear understanding of what you are paying for. Facebook, Amazon and Google offer reasonable and targeted advertising. Goodreads and RGBookworld do this for free. Other services charge a monthly fee per title.

8. **Complimentary Copies**
   "You get nothing for nothing." Rest assured if the agreement with the publisher states that you are getting complimentary copies, you are paying for them as part of the "package." You are also paying for complimentary copies they may distribute to others.
9. **Retailer Previews**
   This is a good one. Here an author is offered to be set up with Google Book Preview, Amazon Look Inside and other free services. The cost with one agency ranges from $900 upwards.

10. **Awards & Recognition**

   Besides sales, this is something everyone craves. Winning an award for a title can certainly increase sales. Then again, there are awards and there are awards. There are entry fees for some awards and care must be taken as these may far exceed any value gained.
11. **Proofs**
   Yes, you need to see a proof before publishing. You will need to pay for a proof of your finished book. Depending on size and other parameters, KDP will charge what it costs to produce it; say about $5 plus shipping. Any more and you may be paying above the odds.
12. **Social Media**
   Social media costs nothing to set up. It does cost some time. If you are unclear on how to do this, you will want to engage and pay someone to do it for you. The same applies to actively posting and responding. You can also employ your 14-year-old neighbour.

13. Author Page on Agency Site

As discussed, you need an author page or pages on high value, reputable sites with a lot of users. We would question what kind of traffic might come to an agency site and why you might want to pay them for this.

14. Reviews

Yes, of course you need and want book reviews. Friends and family are your first approach and they are free. Well, you will have to give them a copy of your book – print or eBook. Have them post their reviews on Amazon and Goodreads – which is free. If you need help getting reviews, or want a prominent person, you may indeed have to pay a nominal amount.

15. Editing, Type, Design & Layout

As discussed at length earlier, these are indeed must-haves. They are something you may be able to do yourself. You may also know someone who will help you or you can opt to hire a free-lance editor or artist. If you engage someone to work with you, be they an individual or an agency, ensure you know up-front what their skill level is and what they will be charging you.

Co-branded Books, A Very Effective Marketing Tool

There are several ways in which a company can positively impact its business and strengthen customer relationships. One important and oft overlooked way is for them to find a non-fiction or even a fiction book relevant to their product offering. Then working with its author/publisher they make it their own by adding their brand and marketing message to it.

Why co-brand a book?

Anyone can have their logo printed on a T-shirt, pen, mug, or mouse mat, but a book is unique. It contains knowledge. Co-branding provides your corporate partner with an economical way of giving their customers a uniquely styled and very appropriate gift. Other terms used for this are custom publishing, content marketing, branded content, co-promotion, brand partnership, brand alliance, etc.

Non-fiction, paperback books are perhaps among the most cost-effective and long-lasting premium products a company can use to build their business. Books are generally kept for long periods of time. They carry a higher perceived value than many other less personal products. People rarely throw out a book – particularly if its content is relevant to them.

The custom published book is one of today's most effective business strategies in reaching targeted groups of people with information relevant to their needs, interests and lifestyles. The strength of a book's inherent permanence can maximize your partner's marketing dollars with a message that endures.

All of our books are available for co-branding, which means that the entire cover design can be changed to match our partner's corporate identity. Alternatively, they may wish to add just their logo to the front cover or they may work out a deal where the entire contents allude to their product or service offering.

An example of one of our co-branded titles

Book Sales

Your first approach to selling books in today's world, must be creating a demand for your title. Make sure you have a good and strong platform. Ensure that people in your target audience know who you are and that you are the expert. If you have other interests, build on these to create a big footprint. Within that ensure that all the elements are interconnected. That way, anyone who comes in contact with you or something you have produced will be exposed to your other work.

Many self-published authors, having produced a worthy book, have gotten a 'leg-up' by printing a quantity of books, going from shop to shop and selling their books one at a time. If you live in a big city, this may indeed be an option. For anyone out in the country, it may not be.

Sales Models (€ $ £)

Traditional Publishing

As mentioned previously, a publisher offered us a contract to purchase our book on boat anchoring. In fact, it was a whopping $10,000. At the time we parted company primarily because of his desire to change the title. As you will see from the following cost and earnings examples, our decision may indeed have been good for another reason as well.

How to book: 352 pages 6x9"

- List price **$29.95**
- Publisher offered us **$10,000 advance** (= € 9,000)
    - Gross revenue per book by publisher $18.00
    - Printing cost $ 3.00
    - Editing, Marketing, Warehousing, and Distribution $ 5.00
    - Net profit/Book $10.00
    - Royalty at 10% of profit
    - **Our Royalty/Book** **$ 1.00**

The publisher had stated that he would be printing 10,000 copies. If he had sold the 10,000 copies and if he had decided to do another printing, we may have seen additional royalties.

Taking the calculation a small step further, if he had been able to sell 1,000 copies a year, it would have taken ten years for him to sell his stock. By then we would have been long overdue for a new edition as there were many changes in the marketplace.

As it happened, we brought out the second edition of the book two years later because there were too many updates for us to ignore. As of this writing, we are well into the third edition only eight years into the life of this title.

Short run book printing (Self-Publishing)

As also mentioned, once we came to the decision to go it on our own and self-publish, we printed a batch of books in my printing company. So, here is how the costs and earnings worked out:

How to book: 352 pages 6x9"

• List price	**$29.95**
• Print 250 copies $2000 (each:)	$ 8.00
• Postage (natl. & UK)	$ 6.00
• Postage (intl.)	$16.00
• Packaging & delivery to PO	$ 8.00

• Net, natl. (~30% of sales)	$ 8.95
• Net (intl.) (~70% of sales)	-$ 2.05

• Blended together perhaps	**+- $ 0.00**

In reality, we did not personally pay for the printing and bindery of the books. Still, once we had factored in the time we spent selling and getting the books out the door, we were barely breaking even.

So, it was time for plan "C."

Print on Demand (Self-Publishing)

With our printing company having competed against Lightning Source for years as a short run book printer, we understood how POD worked. As it happened, we went with KDP, an Amazon company, purely because they did not require any form of contract or exclusivity and there were no upfront costs. The latter was the main driver in our decision making.

How to book: 352 pages 6x9"

- List price **$29.95**
- Royalty
    - Amazon.com ($) $12.90
    - Amazon.co.uk (£) $ 9.19
    - Amazon EU (€) $10.24
    - Expanded Distribution $ 6.91

Blended together = perhaps $10 royalty per book

Sell 20/month => 240 books/year

=> **$ 2,400/year net**

As is readily evident see, if you sell any books at all, even just one copy, you will generate revenue. Although the royalties we have earned do not come to a lot on an annual basis, we have, by now, earned more money from our book than the publisher had offered us for it. Every penny we make from here on is profit – mind you we have spent countless hours on the second and third editions, but that is, shall we say, something we thoroughly enjoyed doing. Besides, by keeping this book up-to-date, it remains something we can be proud of. And, by being up to date, it will continue to sell.

Working with Distributors and Resellers

If you are self-publishing and going to go for a model other than Print on Demand, then how your book will be distributed is something you need to think about. As mentioned earlier, with the first edition of our first book, we did all the mailing and fulfilment ourselves.

If you do choose to work with a reseller, book store, or a major distributor, you must treat your relationship as a business. They are not doing you a favour by taking on your book. They are doing it solely to make money. Consequently, you must be professional in your handling of your paperwork. You, too, want to make money.

A **distributor** will often have an online presence to sell books directly. They also work with and place books on a sale or return basis with resellers or book shops. They will often ask for larger quantities of books, if the title suits their market.

A **book shop** sells a wide range of titles. Because of this, they cannot stock more than one or two copies of each, unless the title is a proven best-seller.

Collateral material

When we delivered some books to one of our resellers, he expressed amazement when we handed him a complete set of paperwork to go with them; including an invoice. None of the prior self-published authors had had anything for him on the first day. Their books had thus languished in boxes until he had all the information in hand.

If you have not done so already, create a **headed notepaper** template. This does not need to be fancy, but should have all your contact information on it, as well as your company name or business name, should you have one. If you have a logo, great; if not, no worries.

Using your notepaper as a basis, set up a **commercial invoice** template. This should include VAT or sales tax if you are registered. It can be done in either Word or in Excel – the latter incorporating all the calculations you need. There are templates available for this online.

A reseller will expect a **40% discount** on your recommended retail price. This discount should be clearly displayed on your invoice.

A catalogue reseller will require a **listing information sheet** for each title. A book shop will also appreciate this very much. The listing information sheet should include the following information:

- Book title
- Book Description (long and short)
- Keywords
- ISBN[43]
- Author biography
- Length in pages and dimensions
- Date of publication

When working with book shops and resellers you will need to keep a quantity of books on hand to replenish their stocks. It will also be up to you to monitor their stocking level, just as any publisher's salesperson has to do. Any one of these may literally have thousands of titles on their list. They cannot, or more probably will not, pay attention to the quantity on hand of an individual title – bar the best sellers.

If you just work with a couple of local resellers, then ordering a few at a time through KDP will suffice. If you wish to work with a larger distributor, you may have to revisit short run printing (and obtaining your own ISBN).

One issue you will invariably face when working with any reseller is getting paid. A business will typically expect 30-45 days' credit (after they have sold the book); more, much more, if they can get away with it. In the publishing business some will also work on a sale or return basis. If they do not sell and get paid-for your

[43] Remember that the ISBN assigned to your title by KDP belongs to them. You are not permitted to use it for sales outside of Amazon. The same applies to Smashwords. For more information on obtaining an ISBN, see the appendix.

book, they will not pay you. Worse still, if a book is damaged, irrespective of by whom, it becomes your problem.

Final Words

Hopefully we've given you enough to point you in the right directions.

Every book deserves to be published;
even if you are the only one to read it.

You never know, the next blockbuster may be the one you've been sitting on. So, get to work, there's much to get done. If we can do it, so can you.

"...Life is about the people you meet and the things you create with them, so go out and start creating. Life is short, live your dream and wear your passion."

From the Holstee Manifesto

Dear Reader:

Thank you very much for purchasing

Self-Publishing for Success

Every book deserves to be published

Second Edition

by

Alex Blackwell

www.WhiteSeahorse.ie

We truly hope that it has helped you with your own work

We greatly value your opinion. Please be kind enough to post your thoughts about it on www.amazon.com and goodreads.com

PS: if you have a story to tell about your publishing success, do please share

Appendix

POD Resources

Espresso Book Machine

An interesting service that has been slow to take off is the Xerox® **Espresso Book Machine™** or EBM. This is a compact book-printing kiosk that can be installed in a bookshop or public place to print, bind and cut books on demand while the customer waits. It allows bookshops to offer their customers almost immediate access to a wider range of titles than could be held onsite. Although Xerox discontinued production of the EBM, it is understood that there are currently two manufacturers developing new book machines of this type.

CreateSpace (= BookSurge), now KDP

Amazon purchased BookSurge and rebranded it as CreateSpace having acquired their customer base and programming. These features have now been ported over to KDP (Kindle Direct Publishing). CreateSpace has been deactivated.

KDP (Kindle Direct Publishing)

KDP are eBook (Kindle) publishers and book printers and publishers. Working with KDP is very easy. They will not contact you unless you ask them to. You are never under any pressure or obligation. KDP has a reputation for a high standard of service. You can choose how you want to use the service. It can be entirely free, or you can pay for what you need. There is no contract or any commitment and no upfront cost. Book sales are through Amazon. You will find more information on KDP in the chapter *Selling your eBook Online Using KDP.*

Amazon has multiple book printing facilities worldwide. This is a network that is sure to increase in years to come.

Lightning Source

Lightning Source is a business unit of Ingram Content Group, which has the industry's largest active book inventory with access to 7.5 million titles. The markets they serve include booksellers, librarians, educators and specialty retailers. Ingram Content Group is a major distributor for independent book stores. Lightning Source are book printers and publishers. They have facilities in Tennessee, Pennsylvania, Ohio, California, United Kingdom, France and Australia. They also provide full service distribution including sales and marketing services via the Ingram Publisher Services division.

Lightning Source provide a wide range of paid services. They require a contract and a commitment. If you register on their site, you should expect a sales person to phone you. All you need to get started is an email address, print-ready PDFs for print titles, EPUB and JPEG for eBooks, an ISBN and a credit card. Books are sold on Amazon, Barns & Noble and eBook channels.

LuLu

Lulu has a good reputation for its online book publishing services. The site clearly explains the guidelines for publishing, so you know exactly what you are buying if or when you pay for a service. It offers package deals and individual services. There is no contract or any commitment and no upfront cost. Book sales are through Barns & Noble, Amazon and other eBook channels.

Outskirts Press

Outskirts Press offer a range of basic services, as well as modern marketing options. They require a non-refundable down payment fee for upfront information, which includes the costs for their services. Outskirts Press can format your book for the Amazon Kindle for an extra fee and can create and distribute a professional book trailer. They also provide an author page and an online bookstore. They use Ingram Book Group and Baker & Taylor as distributors. They sell through Amazon, Buy.com and the websites for Barnes & Noble, Powell's, Alibris and AbeBooks.

AuthorHouse

AuthorHouse provide a wide range of paid-for services. Besides the usual editing and design services this includes marketing services, book trailers and personal appearances. They also do eBook conversion and sales. If you register on their site you should expect a sales person to phone you. Among online publishing companies, AuthorHouse is said to have the largest number of titles in print. Self-

publishing your book through AuthorHouse typically takes 12 to 18 weeks from start to finish. Book sales are through Barns & Noble and Amazon.

iUniverse

iUniverse provide a wide range of paid-for services. They also offer a range of paid marketing services in case you do not have the experience to market your book. These services include help from a personal publicist, press releases and assistance in arranging public appearances. They help you get an author website. They have distribution relationships with both Ingram Book Group and Baker & Taylor. iUniverse also have an online bookstore. They also sell through Amazon, Barnes & Noble, Buy.com, Powell's, Alibris and AbeBooks.

Breezeway Books

Breezeway Books, also known as Llumina Press, offer a free initial editorial evaluation to determine how much, if any, editing your manuscript might need. They offer a range of paid service packages. It takes about 12 weeks to bring a manuscript to a finished format. They work with the distributors Ingram Book Group and Baker & Taylor. Breezeway Books have an online bookstore and also sell your book on Amazon, BarnesandNoble.com, Buy.com, Powells.com, Alibris.com and AbeBooks.com.

Xlibris

Xlibris offer a wide range of paid services and packages. They provide an author page and a book page on their website. It takes 12 to 17 weeks to get your book from manuscript into published form. They distribute their books through the Ingram Book Group. In addition to Xlibris' online store, you can sell your book through Amazon, BarnesandNoble.com, Buy.com, Powells.com, Alibris.com and AbeBooks.com.

Virtual Book Worm Publishing

Virtual Book Worm Publishing offer publication packages with relatively low costs. They do Kindle conversion and book trailers. They can take your book from editing to printed form in four to six weeks. They sell through Baker & Taylor and Ingram Book Group distributors. Your book can also be sold through Virtual Book Worm's online bookstore, Amazon, BarnesandNoble.com, Buy.com, Powells.com, Alibris.com and AbeBooks.com.

Infinity Publishing

Infinity Publishing offer a number of paid packages. They do eBook conversions for an additional fee. They offer a no-risk opportunity for book retailers to sell your book. Bookstores can stock your book with the knowledge that they can return any unsold copies. It takes six to nine weeks to work through the process from manuscript to finished book. You must pay extra to get your book sold through the distributors Ingram Book Group and Baker & Taylor. You have options to sell through Infinity's online store, Amazon, Buy.com, BarnesandNoble.com, Powells.com, Alibris.com and AbeBooks.com.

Wheatmark

Wheatmark offer an array of paid editing, publishing and marketing services as well as a paid editorial evaluation. It typically takes about 12 weeks to bring a title from manuscript to a finished book. Wheatmark use the distributors Ingram Book Group and Baker & Taylor. Wheatmark have an online bookstore and you can sell your book through Amazon, BarnesandNoble.com, Buy.com, Powells.com, Alibris.com and, AbeBooks.com.

Photo Book Resources

- AdoramaPix
- Albelli
- Blurb
- Mixbook
- Mycancvas
- Ofoto
- Photobook America
- Picaboo
- PrestoPhoto
- Shutterfly
- Snapfish
- Walgreens Photo
- Walmart Photo

EBook Resources

- Kindle (Amazon - mobipocket)

    - File: .prc, .mobi, .azw
    - Amazon sites worldwide
- Smashwords – will convert your title and distribute it to a number of major resellers
    - iBook (Apple – ePub3)
        - File: .ibooks
        - iStore, iTunes
    - Nook (Barnes & Noble – ePib)
        - File: .epub
        - BarnsandNoble.com
- Pdf (Adobe)
    - File: .pdf
    - Open platform, Acrobat Reader (free) https://get.adobe.com/reader/
- Adobe Digital Editions
    - Most major publishers use Adobe Digital Editions (ADE) to proof-read their books. Download this free eReader to experience your books in the most optimum format across PC, MAC, tablets or mobile devices. http://www.adobe.com/solutions/eBook/digital-editions.html

Editing Resources

Editorial Freelancers Association (US)

EFA members are editors, writers, indexers, proof-readers, researchers, desktop publishers, translators and others. http://www.the-efa.org/

Common rates:
http://www.the-efa.org/res/rates.php

The Society for Editors and Proof-readers (UK)

SfEP is a professional organisation for editors and proof-readers. https://www.sfep.org.uk/

Common rates:
https://www.sfep.org.uk/resources/suggested-minimum-rates/

www.Writing.ie (IRL)

This is an online magazine site for writers and readers of all ages. They have a listing of editors.

ISBN

The International Standard Book Number is a unique product identifier for books and related material. Whilst it is not a legal requirement to allocate ISBNs to your books, it is used by publishers, booksellers and libraries for ordering, listing and stock control purposes. It enables them to identify a particular publisher and allows the publisher to identify a specific edition of a specific title in a specific format within their output. Systems used by publishers, booksellers and libraries all rely on the ISBN to identify books ensuring they select and stock the correct title and edition.

There are two places the ISBN needs to be put:

- On the back cover in barcode format
- In the front matter in numerical format

ISBNs for British and Irish publishers are issued (for a charge) by the UK International Standard Book Numbering Agency: Nielsen UK ISBN Agency.

A single ISBN currently costs £89. They may also be purchased in bulk for considerably less.

https://www.nielsenisbnstore.com/

In the US, ISBNs are managed by Bowker. A single ISBN currently costs $125. They may also be purchased in bulk for considerably less.

http://www.isbn.org/

Although either of the above will charge extra for the ISBN barcode you will need for your book, if you search for "ISBN barcode generator," you will find several free and easy to use resources online.

Note: KDP and Smashwords provide free ISBNs.

Commercial Digital Audio Workstations (DAW)

This information is from Wikipedia and may be incomplete.

- Ableton Live
- ACID Pro
- Adobe Audition
- Ardour
- Audiotool
- Bitwig Studio
- Cakewalk SONAR
- Caustic
- Digital Performer
- FL Studio
- Fairlight
- GarageBand
- Kristal

- Logic Pro
- Lumit
- Maschine
- MAGIX Samplitude
- MAGIX Sequoia
- Mixcraft
- Mixbus
- MuLab (MuTools)
- MusE
- n-Track Studio
- Synapse Orion
- PreSonus Studio One
- Pro Tools
- Pyramix
- REAPER
- Renoise
- Reason
- SAWStudio
- Steinberg Sequel
- Steinberg Cubase
- Steinberg Nuendo
- Tracktion
- Zynewave Podium
- Z-Maestro

About Alex Blackwell

Alex was a co-owner of a commercial printing company which included a short-run book printing division. They targeted run lengths from 50 to 1,000 copies of premium quality, perfect bound (soft-cover) and case bound (hard-cover) books. These were produced for individual authors, publishers and book marketing firms.

Since then, he and his wife Daria have written and self-published several novels and non-fiction books. All their titles are available in print and digital format. Alex does the design, layout and prep for the final files. He also does the publishing, including the conversion to Kindle and other eBook[44] formats.

Leveraging social media, their informational and publishing websites and public speaking engagements, one of their titles has become the best seller in its genre on Amazon. As their author footprint grows, so does the traction of their overall published portfolio.

In addition to this book, Alex does one-hour workshops as well as an adult education course on self-publishing. As with this book, the objective of the course is to teach the participants how to correctly format their manuscript as a book and design their own book cover using tools on their own laptop and online. Participants are then taught how to set up their account and publish

---

[44] An electronic book (eBook or e-book) is a book publication made available in digital form. It consists of text, images, or both and is readable on computers or other electronic devices.

their book on sites such as Amazon. In addition, they learn how to get their books printed in small quantities on equipment such as the Electronic Book Machine (EBM) or in larger quantities with a commercial printer.

Also Available from White Seahorse Publishing

The Butterfly Effect; It started on 9/11

Book 1 of the Butterfly Effect Series

By Alex Blackwell

The Butterfly Effect has been described as an *'addictive page turner'*. Once you pick it up you will find it hard to put down again.

September 11, 2001 will forever be etched into people's minds as 9/11. The intent was clearly to bring down the United States of America. But the momentum of the American machine is simply too great for an isolated event to bring it to its knees. Or is it?

Jason Geraghty lost his beloved wife on 9/11. She was working for a secret government agency in the north tower of the World Trade Center. In the certainty that this was the third and penultimate time the US Government had wronged him, his mission in life became creating an event that would actually bring down America.

Also from White Seahorse Publishing

The Brotherhood; Acquisition of Power

Book 2 of the Butterfly Effect Series

By Alex Blackwell

Blending current events with historical fiction, *The Brotherhood* is a book you will want to read in one sitting!

The sinking of the German Reich's greatest Battleship, the *Bismarck*, after a mere eight days at sea on her first assignment triggered a series of events that empowered the Bayer family to build a powerful business empire and create a brotherhood of like-minded German industrialists. Developing technology gives them the resources to acquire power greater than most countries in an audacious move. With this as a threat, world domination is in sight. However, the youngest of the Bayer dynasty, sees things differently: power must be used to be effective.

Dragged out of retirement, Jack O'D, who saved humanity in book 1 of the Butterfly Effect series, recruits Peter Blessingham, an ingenious computer hacker, into the biggest and most secretive intelligence-gathering organization in the world.

Can Peter and his team thwart the Brotherhood in their efforts? Can he stop the end of the world as we know it from happening?

Also from White Seahorse Publishing

Sean

Book 3 of the Butterfly Effect series

By Alex Blackwell
Available 2019

Sean follows the story of the younger Blessingham brother, Sean. He makes some bad decisions, which have unexpected negative results. Thc excitement starts in the very first chapter, where a sailing trip on a lovely classic yacht goes horribly awry.

During this time his path crosses with that of Wolfgang Bayer, head of a secret society of Teutonic lineage. This society is in the process of taking its final, ultimately violent step towards German world domination.

Jack O'D is brought out of retirement to recruit the Irish-American Blessingham brothers as cybersecurity wizards, pitting them against Bayer in a struggle to avert his seizing the ultimate control. Both sides use actually available technology on a global scale, making this a very realistic and exciting story – one that might be unfolding today.

As with the first two books in the *Butterfly Effect Series*, this is a fast-paced thriller you will want to keep reading.

Also from White Seahorse Publishing

Oyster Delight

By Alex Blackwell
with illustrations by John Joyce

"The definitive guide to enjoying oysters"

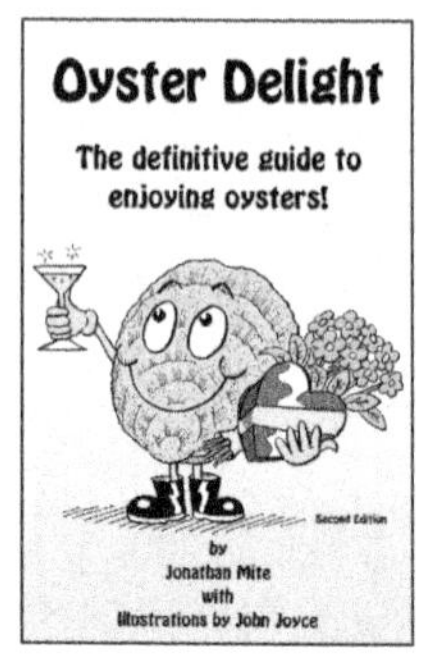

There has never been an oyster cookbook like this one, guaranteed. It covers just about everything an oyster lover would care to learn about this delectable little devil.

Written by a marine biologist who started an oyster hatchery in the West of Ireland and originally used a version of the cookbook to boost sales, it eventually grew to become this entertaining and most extraordinary, definitive guide to everything about oysters. It is eminently readable, not like a cookbook at all, but informative and entertaining.

Also from White Seahorse Publishing

Cruising the Wild Atlantic Way

By Daria & Alex Blackwell

The guide to the beauty and amenities of Ireland's Wild Atlantic West Coast

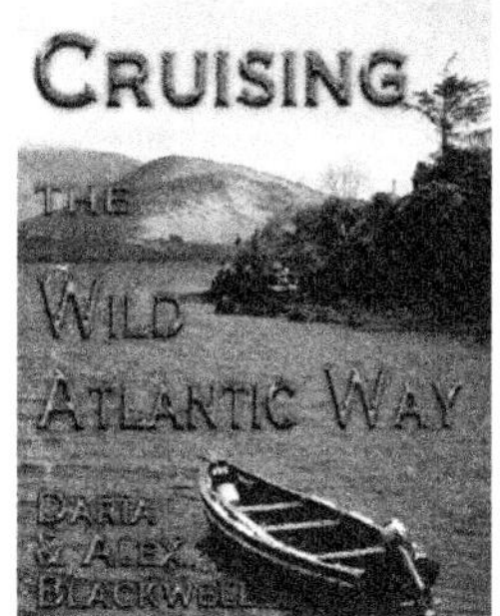

Whether travelling by road or boat, experience the true Ireland.

Ireland's untamed West Coast dotted with islands is one of the most challenging and daunting coastlines to sail. It can also be among the most rewarding if the weather cooperates and the mariner is well prepared for cruising this remote stretch of ocean. This island nation sits out in the North Atlantic which can stir up powerful fury and provide unbelievable beauty.

Find out what it takes to sail the Wild Atlantic Way. Learn the secrets of how to prepare, where to stop and how to thoroughly enjoy this unique and stunning cruising ground. Stretching from Donegal to Cork, it is the most unspoiled stretch of coastline in Europe. See a land as it was seen by explorers centuries ago; in a time when roads didn't exist and the sea was the means by which to travel.

Visit www.whiteseahorse.ie for more information

Also from White Seahorse Publishing

Happy Hooking – the Art of Anchoring

By Alex & Daria Blackwell

Happy Hooking is a very readable book loaded with valuable information on anchoring tackle, anchoring technique, tying up and rafting, anchoring etiquette, as well as the occasional anecdote - simply stated a must have! (If we don't say so ourselves.)

If you could take only one piece of advice from these pages with you on your travels, perhaps you will remember what Tommy Moran, an old salt in the West of Ireland, advised time and again:

"Anchor as though you plan to stay for weeks, even if you intend to leave in an hour."

"The definitive textbook on the subject." Ocean Cruising Club

"It should be mandatory reading for novice sailors and charter operators would do well to place copies throughout their fleet." Cruising Club of America

"It is hard to imagine a more comprensive study of the topic. This is a remarkably easy book to read." Irish Cruising Club

Visit www.whiteseahorse.ie for more information

Also from White Seahorse Publishing

Onyx: The Cruising Kitty

By Daria and Alex Blackwell

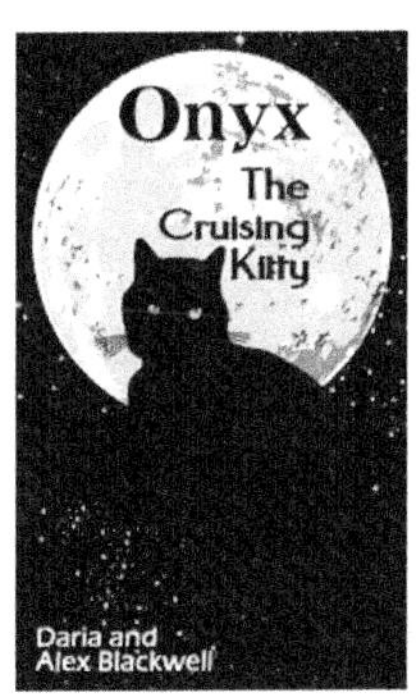

Onyx: The Cruising Kitty is a charming series of chronologically sorted short stories told in the voice of *Onyx* herself. In them she describes her adventures starting with when she chose her 'People.' She tells about how she got her sea legs and became a seafaring cruising kitty. Onyx probably has more sea miles under her paws than most sailors would ever dream of. She crossed the Atlantic three times and visited countless countries along the way.

The book is for all ages. It is easily read. It may be dipped into whenever the reader is in need of an uplifting story or devoured in one sitting.

"I'm Onyx, the Cruising Kitty.
I'm going to see the world.
But first I'll have to take a nap."

Also from White Seahorse Publishing

The Naked Truth
A nautical murder mystery

By Daria Blackwell

Jessica and Xander sailed off in search of adventure. Sailing across oceans on their own boat was exactly the kind of restorative voyage the Lynches craved. They quit their high-powered jobs, sold their house and cast off the lines.

But their adventure sets Jessica on the course of a murder trail. On finding no evidence – no bodies, no signs of struggles – their quest to answer unasked questions begins. Tormented by helplessness, Jessica experiences bizarre dreams within which lay the clues that evaded the professionals.

Intriguing twists of plot are served up in exotic island settings as sailors Jessica and Xander Lynch try to uncover the naked truth behind the trail of murders they encounter.

The Naked Truth is set in the Atlantic Islands and the Caribbean. The description of crossing oceans as a lifestyle is based on the author's experience. Everything else is fiction.

Printed in Great Britain
by Amazon